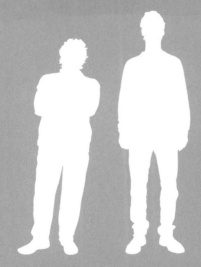

Dietwee / New Dutch Graphic Design

BIS Publishers, Amsterdam 2002

Publisher
BIS Publishers, Amsterdam

Art Direction
Ron Faas, Tirso Francés

Design
Marjolein Spronk, Martine Eelman

Texts
Gert Staal, Staal & De Rijk Editors,
Amsterdam

Translation, editing
Mari Shields, Amsterdam
Jane Bemont, Amsterdam

Photo/Lithography
Bas Wilken

Production Coordination
Maikel van der Laken

Printer
Grafisch Bedrijf Tuijtel,
Hardinxveld-Giessendam

Binder
Callenbach, Nijkerk

BIS Publishers
Herengracht 370-372
1016 CH Amsterdam
The Netherlands
T +31 (0)20 5247560
F +31 (0)20 5247557
bis@bispublishers.nl
www.bispublishers.nl

Dietwee
Kruisdwarsstraat 2
3581 GL Utrecht
The Netherlands
T +31 (0)30 2343555
F +31 (0)30 2333611
info@dietwee.nl
www.dietwee.nl

ISBN 90-72007-86-7

Contents

4   Lasting Virtue of Necessity Born
       Gert Staal

9   The Work
       Ten Years of Dietwee

166   Credits

168   Thanks

Lasting Virtue of Necessity Born

Their collaboration dates back to art college. It was at the academy in Utrecht where Tirso Francés and Ron Faas had met as graphic design students back in 1986. Within a couple of weeks, Francés had climbed up onto a school table to declare himself treasurer of the school's festivities committee. He seemed to view Utrecht as one of countless stops in his trip around the world. Tirso Francés was born in America, the son of a former Spanish priest and a Dutch writer, and had arrived by way of the De Breul boarding school in Zeist in the Netherlands and Belmont Abbey College in Hereford, England. In the mid-1980s, after a brief inspection of the Gerrit Rietveld Academy – 'a lot of students wearing eyeliner and dressed in black' – he decided to move on to Utrecht for his art training. 'I am an odd chameleon and have this manoeuvrability from my catholic background. Actually, I never had the idea of becoming a graphic designer. I was destined for journalism. Because of the early specialization in English schools and the inspiration of one of my teachers there, I finally decided on graphic design.' He has since remained true to that decision, and Utrecht would become the permanent home of the studio that he would later establish with Ron Faas.

In preparing for his own art school years, Faas meticulously went through all the steps that one envisions for a budding designer: graphics-specialized high school followed by a graphics technical school. From the age of eleven, he knew what he would be doing with his life. It perhaps all fits in with the impression he gives of his background, one of Dutch sobriety, fuelled by the adventure that a new village being built in a freshly reclaimed polder can offer a young boy. Faas used to wander with friends around familiar streets, dig in the mountains of sand on endless building sites and spend every Saturday morning on the local football field. It is a classic, ultimately Dutch décor, of the kind film director Alex van Warmerdam reconstructed to perfection in the film 'De Noorderlingen' (The Northerners). 'For Ron, everything beyond the dyke at the edge of his village seemed like a foreign country,' quips his partner.

This combination of temperaments is uncommon, at the very least. It is precisely this synthesis of daring and sound dependability, pragmatism, fun and analysis that gives the work of Dietwee a place of its own in Dutch graphic design, not as a representative of any given style or design philosophy, but sooner through a salutary lack thereof.

The collaboration was born after the two very different students had spent some six months in contact with one another and had become friends. Where the one was earning a decent wage by filling petrol tanks in his free time, the other was already suffering under the weight of more design commissions than he could handle. In the evenings, Ron Faas was designing advertisements and quite simply needed help to meet the demand. Alongside their school work, the two developed a blossoming – if limited – professional studio. It was sufficiently professional that they could allow themselves the luxury of a Mac Plus and a disk drive while they were still in school. This was then a digital magic lantern that had just been introduced to the Utrecht academy by teacher Max Kisman, but which would still count on broad-scale distrust from the established design world.

This was not so for Tirso Francés. 'Printing out on a real typesetter – that was difficult. To do that, we still had to drive to Amersfoort, 35 kilometers from here. With Max, we saw how quickly you could draw in frames, how efficiently you could set type. We looked at our Mac as a tool, like a new Rotring pen. I didn't much notice all those limitations that other people were so afraid of. Suddenly you did not need to make working drawings and – unlike Ron – I was notoriously bad at them. Whether you could really produce top quality classic typography with a computer was a discussion we preferred to avoid.'

Not long afterwards, they were asked by the academy to familiarize their fellow students with designing on the computer. They also advised the first converts amongst the teachers about their own purchase of an Apple Macintosh computer and its use, thus unexpectedly becoming travelling salesmen for hardware and software products. Francés continues, 'I advised some of our role models – Irma Boom, Koeweiden Postma and Mart Warmerdam, whose class I was attending the next day.' The Apple dealer granted him a five-percent commission. In the land of the blind, for a short while the one-eyed man was king.

Clever Organization
As a proper studio, Dietwee ('Those Two' in Dutch) began taking shape in 1988, 'Actually out of boredom,' explains Tirso Francés. 'We were the class that kept missing the boat when it came to good, new teachers. Max Kisman, Peter Mertens, Henri Lucas, Vincent van Baar, André Toet, they were the people that we just managed to miss.' On the other hand, their 'business' quickly began making demands on them.

'It was so exciting that we took on almost everything. We were often too optimistic, so that we ended up working all night to get the work finished before a deadline,' Ron Faas recalls. 'I remember Ron always complaining during those nights while we were working for a presentation, that the client was at home, peacefully sleeping the night away,' adds Francés. They became accustomed to working within tight budgets, while the results had to be unconditionally good. They realized it was a question of clever organization, and thinking up ingenious, inexpensive solutions. They did their lithographs on the photocopy machine. Light and darker copies were superimposed under the printer's camera. It was a continual learning process, and with it came the pleasure of achieving good results within those minimal margins of error.

It was virtually unavoidable, however, that their schoolwork would suffer. The first bad grade came in their fourth year: 'Finally, we were confronted with the fact that we had been sliding by,' remembers Tirso Francés. That changed, however, in 1990, with a commission from Stylos, a student association at the Technical University in Delft. Faas and Francés were asked to make a design for the School of Architecture's symposium on 'Context & Modernity'.

Francés: 'Without having seen any previous designs, we were told that a brother of one of the students had done it the year before, so we thought we could easily improve on that. Only it turned out that the architecture student was Roemer van Toorn, and the designer they were talking about was his father, Jan van Toorn. That was a bit of a shock, but we absolutely still wanted to do the project.'

They tried to bring the project into the context of the academy, with an eye to receiving some guidance. It was then that the door was shut. The faculty – who had been looking on with mixed feelings as the 'slick kids' were busy setting up their own commercial studio – finally saw their chance. There would be no permission granted to do the project at school. Francés and Faas decided that they would leave school for a semester in order to complete the job, and start their fourth year over again afterwards. To everyone's amazement, they did return to finish their fourth year, as well as complete several more projects. By that time, Dietwee had in fact been a reality for over six months.

Doctrines

When they returned after their eight-month absence, the academy had changed. A new team of teachers had arrived on the scene. Influential younger instructors, such as Menno Landstra and Mart Warmerdam, were now supported by Ronald Timmermans and Pieter Roozen, who viewed the computer as a fully valid, complete instrument of Design. Most of all, they had a different approach to content. Francés speaks of different 'doctrines': the generally accepted doc-

trine of the image you make yourself, as opposed to Warmerdam and Roozens' preference for the 'found' image; Landstra's preference for Garamond in small caps or Warmerdam's sans-serif typography. At that point, there were various 'truths' being simultaneously propagated in design education. From their own communications experience, Faas and Francés knew of yet another – the client and his public.

Once again, another contradiction lies at the root of the design mentality associated with Dietwee. It is not following any doctrine that in fact determines their form, and it takes no effort at all to see this in their work. From their perspective, it is impossible to approach extremely varying commissions from a single professional theory. Time and again, the specific situation will determine which approach is appropriate, how form and communicative effect influence one another and how a client or target group is spoken to. 'At first,' says Francés, 'our thinking is often at odds with the client, not because we already have the answer waiting, but because we actually begin on an assignment with as blank a slate as possible. It is not to undermine him, either. This researching and questioning of an assignment is meant to clarify what the actual question is. If that succeeds, there is a wide open space in which to design and we are consequently able to be more receptive to the wishes of the client.'

In the same way that the work is not guided by any doctrine whatsoever, neither Faas nor Francés have any interest in manning their studio with mirror images of themselves. For a long while now, Dietwee has no longer been simply synonymous with its founders. The face of the studio is also shaped by designers such as Robin Uleman, who left Philips Design in 1998 to work in Utrecht. Dietwee, Francés declares, offers a place for very different personalities and ideas about design. At most, there is one major common denominator. 'We intentionally cast the staff of the studio across a wide range of frequencies, but the heart of the matter is their approach to design communication. What we are all good at is translating, turning a question into a design and a story that insists on people paying attention, that makes contact.'

Leafing through the many annual reports, brochures, flyers, books, house styles, websites and posters that Dietwee have made over the years, that principle becomes crystal clear. In the final result, Dietwee do not try to intensify problems, but to communicate. The studio is not playing with its own identity, but clarifying that of the client. The magic lies in the immediate attraction of design and narrative, not in any intellectual rehashing by viewers 'in the know'.

Beauty

'Beauty is something we usually say you shouldn't worry about. It will come on its own. You have to watch out for it more than seek it out. And you shouldn't ever complain about it.' (Ron Faas)

Making Things

'The type of work you do keeps coming back to you.' (Tirso Francés)

Direct

'When I worked under Bas Oud, I learned what directness was. His creed was why make things difficult if they can be easy. He coupled speed with an enormously well-developed sense of form.' (Ron Faas)

New

'The design critic Hugues Boekraad once said to us that our studio has the benefit of constant change. If market developments had been evolutionary, then we probably wouldn't have had the chances we have. We reaped the benefits of revolution, of stormy social and technical changes.' (Tirso Francés)

Youth

'The flyers that we sent in for the Rotterdam Design Prize lent form to a subculture. They were naïve. They had to be finished quickly, but they unambiguously associated us with youth culture. A couple of years later, when we were asked to design a postage stamp, that was good news. Recognition at last. But the bad news was that a postage stamp for young people had just been issued. Dietwee was commissioned to make a stamp for the Senior Citizens Union, because the Dutch Post Office wanted them to appeal more to young people.' (Ron Faas)

Genes

'When we moved to our new address, an old factory in the centre of Utrecht, we also had to find a new balance. The ship was sailing, but we did not quite know where we were supposed to be headed. Still, there has always been something in the genes of this studio. Through the people we selected, mostly young people, we kept tabs on the atmosphere. And it sounds crazy, but the bigger we became, the more loosely we were able to handle it.' (Tirso Francés)

Video Wall

During the time that Ron Faas and Tirso Francés were doing work-study with Roozen and Timmermans, the Association of Dutch Designers, BNO (Beroepsorganisatie Nederlandse Ontwerpers), held a competition for the design of an exhibition of the best work of student graphic designers. With Roozen and Timmermans' guidance, the two formulated a proposal. For the project, they asked each of twenty state-appointed final exam mentors to nominate a single student completing his or her final project. After a difference of opinion on procedure, Faas and Francés decided not to enter their proposal. Without their knowing about it, however, the school submitted their proposal, and it won.

There was then considerable pressure from the school for them to complete the project, which included the exhibition and an accompanying book. 'Our reaction,' says Faas, 'was that we wanted nothing to do with it! We felt cheated. But if we agreed to it, we would be able to design an exhibition with a video wall in the Stedelijk Museum in Amsterdam… It was difficult to remain true to our principles.'

Their determination took yet a deeper dive when it became clear that both of them – and Francés had already fallen a semester behind – would be able to graduate with this as their final exam project. A reduction of the budget from € 100,000 to € 20,000 was the final enticement they needed to turn them around. Now it had really become an interesting project.

In Amsterdam's Stedelijk Museum, Faas completed a video wall with interviews in which the selected students discussed their work and their mentors explained why they had made their selections. The exhibition was mounted on bales of recycled paper, suggesting the fleeting nature of the profession (a fellow student also worked on this design). The accompanying catalogue designed by Tirso Francés illuminated the relative nature of the profession by juxtaposing the student work with images from the news of the year they graduated. Francés: 'I had to make the book in such a short time that apart from a few sketches, nobody had been able to look at it beforehand. In retrospect, you can see influences from Mart and Pieter, but even they had hardly seen it. The presentation at the opening was a fantastic surprise for everybody!' And the two were graduates at last.

File Folders

The deal that finished their studies also set the pace for picking up where the Dietwee studio had left off. Francés and Faas were by now well initiated and could trust one another implicitly. They also had the equipment. 'We just needed to rent a space and we could get stuck in.' They did a lot of work for a communications agency and made flyers for Hardbop, a series of events organized by friends from the academy. In times of need, designer friends would join them. Richard van der Laken, Harmen Liemburg, and later, Sybren Kuiper, all worked for a time with Dietwee, before starting their own independent studios. As a result, Dietwee became nestled into a network of young kindred spirits, including the Designpolitie (Design Police), GM and Syb Graphic Design, people with whom they still keep close contact. More recently, 178 Aardige Ontwerpers (178 Nice Designers), Hotel, For (New York) and several other studios have also been set up by designers who worked for some time with Dietwee.

In its early days, the studio primarily encountered problems in (over)estimating the possibilities for their clients. Francés: 'We took on everything, just as we had before. We thought we could give a new twist to it all. But with conservative clients, it sometimes fell apart. In the first 18 months, we were mostly occupied with designing things that we thought the client wanted. He could be content, but he wouldn't be surprised. In retrospect, it was not very interesting. That changed when we decided not to work for the communications agency any more and to go out and do what we liked to do. First you decide where you stand, and then with the client, you take it to the limits.'

The clients they then began designing for included the Institut Française de la Mode (IFM) and several small fashion labels, including Stigters and No Fashion. For most of these clients, limited possibilities in colour printing had to be exploited as economically as possible. For this reason, for the IFM Catalogue for example, Faas and Francés in fact delegated a portion of the visual direction to the participating fashion designers. Each was assigned a fixed amount of space in the book for colour and black-and-white lithography, which they could add to or give up by exchanging with each other. The book consequently bore the distinctive personal stamp of each of the participating designers, and was produced as cost-efficiently as possible.

Subsequently, in 1994, when they were a five-man-strong studio, they were approached by BSO/Origin. This multinational software developer, under the inspired leadership of Eckart Wintzen, distinguished themselves from their competition with their unusual annual reports. BSO/Origin had seen the catalogue that Dietwee had made for IFM and were charmed by the inventiveness of the concept. With BSO/Origin, Faas and Francés entered into direct dialogue, and this was the turning point. Suddenly, Dietwee found themselves at the table with a client of considerable weight. Budgets were correspondingly larger and the discussions held directly with company managers and their advertising moved at a hitherto unknown level. Dietwee first completed an internal social report and a few small assignments when, with barely twelve months passed, they were entrusted with BSO/Origin's new annual report. They eventually made the report in the form of a file folder, which almost literally took on the shape of the process of preparation that every annual report undergoes – an apparently unstructured collection of folders, newspaper and memo cuttings, photographs, computer printouts and half-scribbled reminders that are normally resolved by the disciplined order of copywriters and designers. Yet again, virtue had risen of necessity.

Francés: 'BSO/Origin was enthusiastic, but apart from that, things carried on as they were. Without any really serious expectations, we submitted several flyers for the Rotterdam Design Prize, and half a year later, everything was happening at once. The flyers were nominated for the Design Prize and suddenly we were also receiving compliments from former teachers and fellow designers for the BSO/Origin Annual Report, which was subsequently awarded a Golden Lamp by the Art Directors Club of the Netherlands. All at once people really knew who we were. Our success at the corporate level had been added onto the recognition for our flyers, which associated us with youth culture.'

Expanding Scale

The connection with young people meant that Dietwee appealed to such clients as the RABO bank and the Drum Rhythm Festival. As they had been earlier with the introduction of the computer, they were again sent out as pioneers into a territory where they barely knew their way. On the other hand, survival was something Francés and Faas certainly had learned, even if the work flow and the remuneration they received for it left something to be desired. 'For many clients, we were the sexy guys who still didn't cost much, but who'd proven the creativity and success of their work,' Francés explains.

They proved to be an interesting partner for larger studios in discussions and even mergers. In the mid-1990s, long negotiations were held with Qua Associates about a merger that promised success because of the synergy of the respective qualities of the two studios. Qua had great management, lots of work and a well set-up organization which needed creativity on a senior level, and that seemed exactly what Dietwee had to offer. But Faas and Francés were worried about the effect of such a merger on their creative process. In the end, they proved so concerned that after nearly a year of fruitful exchange, they decided to remain independent. At that point, however, they knew one thing for certain. In order to bring in truly interesting work, the studio had to expand and become more professionally organized. A young studio had to become a real studio. Francés: 'For several years, we worked with a mission unknown, afraid we might miss something. Thanks to Qua, we were confronted with the need to be more clear about where we wanted to go.'

Dietwee had just finished their third annual personnel report for BSO/Origin, which was distinguished with the 1996 Annual Reports Award, when ONVZ health insurers knocked at their door. What followed was to become a long-term collaboration. ONVZ promotes themselves with the notion of the human body as our most precious possession, and in their various annual reports and other materials, the designers have continually translated the message anew, with surprising images, texts and forms. Dietwee proved capable of arriving at appealing results not just for BSO/Origin, but for any other company with a desire to stand out and be different.

At just the right time, the ONVZ commission carried the Dietwee ship to rich waters and the studio began its expansion years. The staff of six was doubled, and before long, there were six more. This most recent leap ran parallel with the breakthrough of the Internet. Since that moment, Dietwee has had several full-time interaction designers. Around Christmastime in 2000, there were nearly 30 employees who, pictured as cardboard angels, were mailed around to clients, prospects, friends and acquaintances with the tongue-in-cheek caption, 'Dietwee kan de boom in', which translates loosely as 'Dietwee can go climb a tree'.

In the last few years, a new profile has been taking distinctive shape. Dietwee holds a position as a design studio in the communications industry. Not that it ever took much of a struggle to embrace autonomy in graphic design – a lively and media-genic movement in the Netherlands – but it was the opposite that had to be fought for with the greater strength. Instead of an autistic design philosophy that would have every commission subservient to the personal expression of the designer, Dietwee had to draw their conclusions from the principles with which they approach their clients. How can you interpret and translate the needs of your client and amaze him at the same time? How do you establish as direct as possible a contact with those receiving the information? How can you interfere as little as possible between the sender and the receiver? How do you maximize the effect of your communication while remaining true to your values and ideas?

Questions like these are characteristic of the studio's period of growth, both in terms of the job assignments and the studio staff. Faas and Francés only half comprehended that the strength of their studio was to be found in the exceptional situation that they had created for themselves in such an informal and almost playful manner. Dietwee had actually won an identity without a crystallized design ideology, without a fixed methodology, without the impediment of rules of style. It was precisely this that made them so exceptional.

Their confidence grew. They knew it was possible to penetrate to the core of an assignment, without all the safety nets. Even more importantly, it would perhaps only work when they completely focussed on the analyzing, interpreting and translating of the message that the particular client wanted to disseminate. They were assisted by their great curiosity and aided by the capacity to fish out the essence of the commission without all too many assumptions beforehand, and in lieu of a concrete tale on the client's part, they could construct one for them. Of course, the quality of the work is ultimately bound to the sense of form within the studio, but this is rarely the dominant factor.

In fact, Dietwee follow a well-tried recipe – the designer as telegraph operator. At the same time, however, that early 20th-century metaphor does not entirely hold true. Dietwee is anything but a neutral trap door. Certainly in their work for alternative film houses, parties, festivals and clubs, but also in an annual report for an exclusive bank, the spirit of the times inevitably shines through. Form must ensure that the message is not only signalled on, but is also ingested. Unlike the glory years of Cassandre, designers today undoubtedly have to battle more fiercely and with greater alertness in order to gain the attention of the recipient. What made sense yesterday may be passé tomorrow. Only a short time ago, for example, the use of realistic, snapshot-like photography was a way of expressing a new mentality, a recognizable statement against glossy imagery – although Francés indicates that it their case, the choice was also determined by budgets that did not exactly make slick photography an option. In the meantime, that visual language has moved on to stock photography, and every magazine or advertising agency can acquire them by the hundreds. It will not be long, therefore, before the use of this type of photography has also been worn to the bone.

Space
'There is apparently more space on the Internet than in traditional graphic design, perhaps also because clients cannot really pin you down in the briefing. The Internet adds time, sound and animation. You can simply move more easily.' (Tirso Francés)

Future
'In five years' time, we may no longer exist in this form. Who knows? We might be merged with another company because our qualities cannot grow without their expertise. For me, it is essential that content defines form. Perhaps this is the reason why we have always left whether or not we are just designers or more than that as an open question.' (Ron Faas)

Identity
'Does a ministry of state have a distinct identity? Can it be more than just an outer skin? A uniform? For us, it is only interesting if they want to express who they fundamentally are. No expression without substance. Some studios spend weeks working out details for a corporate coffee cup – then the whole design world is off track. One or two days is more than enough.' (Tirso Francés)

Money
'The budget determines the possibilities. Small budgets have never stopped us from doing what we wanted. We seek the potential within the limitations. We prefer not to even talk about it. However, sometimes money is perhaps important because it is a translation of trust.' (Ron Faas)

Mistakes
'I am happy that I made mistakes. That's where you learn something.' (Tirso Francés)

Reflection

Thinking about the actual development of the studio is not a regular event. There is seldom time to step back and reflect. Production of a book about your own work, however, forces one to take stock. Tirso Francés: 'Ron and I often disagree about crucial decisions. We constantly have to defend our convictions to one another, and that is precisely the strength of our studio. It is a little different now because we have expanded so much. The confrontations are less evident, but when they happen, they can still lead to fantastic results!'

Ron Faas: 'We are not the masters with a bunch of assistants. Everyone is responsible for their own work. We add guidance, serve as the studio mentors, keep badgering about the ingenuity and inventiveness of a technical solution and sometimes serve as 'heavy artillery', accompanying a designer on a visit to a client, but it is no longer simply your own personal thing. We keep track of the flow and the quality. That has to be good.'

Tirso Francés: 'You do not have to do all of the work on a project in order to see it as your own. For certain ideas you have, it is better to ask an outside specialist for a specific style of design or typography, as we did with Syb and Martijn Engelbregt for ONVZ. Advertising agencies have always been better able to understand that. Sometimes I am overcome by a fear that we are not as sharp as we used to be, but our goal is to be very good across the board, rather than outstanding in only a few special areas, the way we were. There are simply to many pans in the fire to depend on any single success, so it is important to work together with other specialists.'

Internal briefings are now set in advance, so that despite the expansion, it is still possible to keep track of the principles in any given commission within the studio. Faas focuses primarily on graphic work and Francés on strategy and Internet activities. Where one operates more impulsively and playfully, the other keeps tabs on the overall line. 'Ron is more intuitive. I am strategic, so I also serve more as an account manager for the whole studio.'

Underbelly Strategy

Faas contends that a project never begins with the design. The starting point lies in assessing the framework of the job, with the intention of creating more space and a better grip on its possibilities. Consequently, a new design for the identity of Planet Internet began with a thorough investigation of the only aspect of the commission that the designers were not allowed to touch – the logo made in 1995.

It is part of Dietwee's strategic approach, especially in the case of larger companies, to seek out the spirit of their client. What they are not allowed to do may be precisely the thing that can reveal the critical gene. Their guide is their practical expertise. Francés calls it 'an underbelly strategy'. 'We do not have a design method. There is no prescribed route or set of rules. But there are no-go areas for us as for anyone else. You only notice it when we are working with designers who are just starting out. Then I suddenly hear myself repeating after my teachers, 'A text has to hang, not stand.' It is at moments like these that the unwritten rules reveal themselves. They are there, but they are not explicit.'

In an attempt to identify the core of their own approach, Ron Faas explains, 'We try to peel our work right back to the essence, not to decorate or obscure anything. We are not purists, but we are also not form freaks. We translate the avant-garde for a larger public. We first bring the tale back to the basics, and then we provide it with a good jacket.'

In part because Dietwee do not shy away from working with the advertising world – for example, KesselsKramer, FHV-BBDO and Lowe – the studio has a reputation for not refusing jobs on moral grounds, a controversial issue in the history of Dutch design. They do, however, contest the causality. The disdain of the established design world for the work of advertising agencies has moreover already generally been very seriously eroded. According to Francés, their contact with KesselsKramer came at just the right moment. KesselsKramer is run by creative thinkers, and for Dietwee, the meeting confirmed that the direction and scale they had chosen for themselves was in fact achievable while still retaining their values, pleasure in their work and high standards. It was indeed possible to design within an environment that could be both corporate and 'fringe'. Their design, when necessary, can share similarities with advertising campaigns, and contribute to the development of brand or company identity.

On the advice of Dietwee, ONVZ entrusted their advertising interests to KesselsKramer, in Amsterdam. A year later, KesselsKramer approached Dietwee to design the house style, brochures and website for the new telecommunications company, Ben. 'Erik Kessels knew that the form and style he was developing for Ben was very close to ours, and that we could help him develop a clear and simple design approach that suited the advertising domain and stood out on its own merits. After KesselsKramer, our own thing had become another thing. By then, for some clients, we were indeed working more as an advertising agency.'

After their initial debut in the Amsterdam Stedelijk Museum, Dietwee had more or less left the established cultural world behind. There was culture enough in their own package of assignments for music festivals, art cinemas and clubs. The official cultural institutions only came back into Dietwee's field of vision with the website they designed for the Mondriaan Foundation. This cultural institute works with established designers such as Irma Boom and Karel Martens for printed matter, but as these designers were not then designing websites, the foundation found Dietwee to be the right studio to translate their identity to the Internet in an original manner. Dietwee liked the assignment. Francés: 'On the Internet, we can easily create a little world of its own for a client. This is perhaps what we love doing most of all – building a communications environment for a brand, company or institution, be it on-line or off-line.'

And the moral side of it?

'Of course we make moral decisions. We were a little hesitant when asked to work for a private investment bank for extremely wealthy clients, but Insinger de Beaufort proved to be both fantastic people and a fantastic client, who in their usually conservative world wanted to stand out and be different, with values they wanted expressed. Last year their annual report highlighted 'masters of their trade'. Everyone, including Ian Kantor, the chief executive, was on hand for the brainstorming sessions we arranged. As had been the case with Eckart Wintzen of BSO/Origin, the collaboration was inspiring and produced one of the best annual reports we ever made.'

'Instead of putting an extra layer of make-up on a client, we prefer first removing all the old make-up, and then touching up only what is needed. If a company or institution truly wants to change their image, then it really does become interesting, but only if they want to change it from the inside out. This gives us the chance to investigate whether they know what they are asking, and whether they are prepared to bear the fundamental consequences of the turnaround. It sounds a little arrogant, perhaps, but in a certain sense, this is a good thing. If asking pertinent questions is regarded as arrogance, it is often what gets the best results.'

Gert Staal (Staal & De Rijk Editors)
(with thanks to Sybren Kuiper and Robin Uleman)

Rijkdom of Ratjetoe

6 7

Op een kunstacademie moet je wel heel veel zelf doen

17

Iets goeds doen met je vak

34 35

De discussie gaat nooit over het nieuwe belastingformulier

Je moet je geen illusies maken over de totale vrijheid

49

Wij zijn de koks van de gelezen tekst

61

Als je niet oppast laten ontwerpers de hele wereld er hetzelfde uitzien

Nieuwe vormen zijn heel vaak opgepoetste clichés

68

Perspective through Confrontation

'Het Oordeel' (The Verdict) was the final exam project with which Ron Faas and Tirso Francés – the founders of Dietwee – graduated from the Utrecht School of the Arts. At most Dutch art academies, graphic designers traditionally graduate with hyper-personal and sometimes even distinctly introverted themes. In their project, Faas and Francés worked under the guidance of teachers Pieter Roozen and Ronald Timmermans with an actual client, the BNO (Association of Dutch Designers); a budget for the assignment (reduced from € 100,000 to € 20,000); and a location (the Stedelijk Museum in Amsterdam). They designed an editorial concept for documenting the work of the twenty best final exam projects within their field through an exhibition and a catalogue. Het Oordeel had to present the work of twenty

different individuals, twenty people who in the previous year had virtually cut themselves off from the outside world in order to complete their projects. In the catalogue, Francés used the metaphor of the introspective design world by contrasting the students' work with news photos from that same year: the Romanian revolution, natural disasters, the victory march of the American Gulf War troops. The photos emphasize the relativity of the designers' concerns, put the profession back into its natural perspective. They used a similar principle (in collaboration with fellow student Maura van Wermeskerken) for the exhibition. On video monitors, Faas showed excerpts from interviews with the students and the external experts who had judged their work during the final exams. The monitors were positioned on

25 pressed bales of old newspapers and advertizing brochures and were partitioned off from the spectators by construction site fencing. The confrontation between 'yesterday's news' and the almost sacred ambitions of their colleagues introduced the sense of perspective Faas and Francés deemed necessary. Designers, Het Oordeel declares, are not the centre of the world and when they are, it doesn't last for long. The exaggerated block shapes of the typography, the harsh contrast between news photos and the students' quotes, the rough stacking of old paper: all these elements are part of the editorial translation of their assignment. A preview of a method that Dietwee is to employ more often in years to come.

WILD STYLE

sunday december 10

HEAVY HARDBOP
G OKT.
HARD BOP

SUNDAY FEBRUARI 11
SPACE FUNK

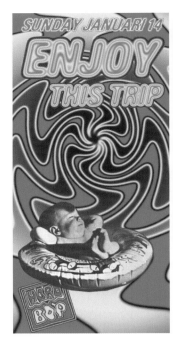

4 YEARS
HARD BOP
SUNDAY NOVEMBER 12

SUNDAY JANUARI 14
ENJOY THIS TRIP

YOU CAN FLY
SUNDAY JUNE 2

SUNDAY NOVEMBER 3
SUBMERGE

EASTER PARADE
EASTER SUNDAY APRIL 7

SUNDAY MARCH 10
FREEDOM

SUNDAY AUGUST 4
HARD BOP
Midsummer-Special
Peace, love & ice-cream

Amazing stuff
Peace, love & ice-cream
sunday september 1

BORN AGAIN!
HARD BOP
(A ONE-TIME-ONLY REUNION)
SUNDAY NOVEMBER 29

HARD BOP
Sunday May 5 Liberation!

SUNDAY JULY 7
REFUNKED!
HARD BOP

HIT IT AND QUIT IT
after 5 years the last HARDBOP!
SUNDAY DECEMBER 1

See the Vibe

In the early nineties, the party circuit in Holland started taking shape. When party art director Arne Koefoed and DJ Frankie D. organized the first Hardbop night – a crossover mix of music styles like Funk, P-Funk, Hiphop, Jazzdance and to a somewhat lesser extent, House – in the Utrecht discotheque Fellini in 1991, a photocopied laser print served as the invitation. The flyer had yet to embark upon its triumphal advance. From that very first night, Dietwee were designers as well as partygoers. Identifying with Hardbop's aspirations proved to be satisfying and easy for them. The flyers were often the result of working together intensively with Koefoed, from whom they learned the subtleties of the various musical genres. They were absorbed in party culture and developed a visual language that was fully in tune with the themes and ideas of the organizers. The flyers always had the same format, with identical reverse sides so that recognition was guaranteed. On the front sides, they experimented for the first time – and thus to the full – with Photoshop, trying out new ideas and converting the music into a graphical code. In the second year, the flyers (most of which are reproduced here) could be printed in two colours. The same printing was therefore used for the virtually abstract typographical flyers for the BoomBoom! parties in Amsterdam's Westergasfabriek, which were devoted to the more experimental Breakbeats, Triphop and early Jungle.

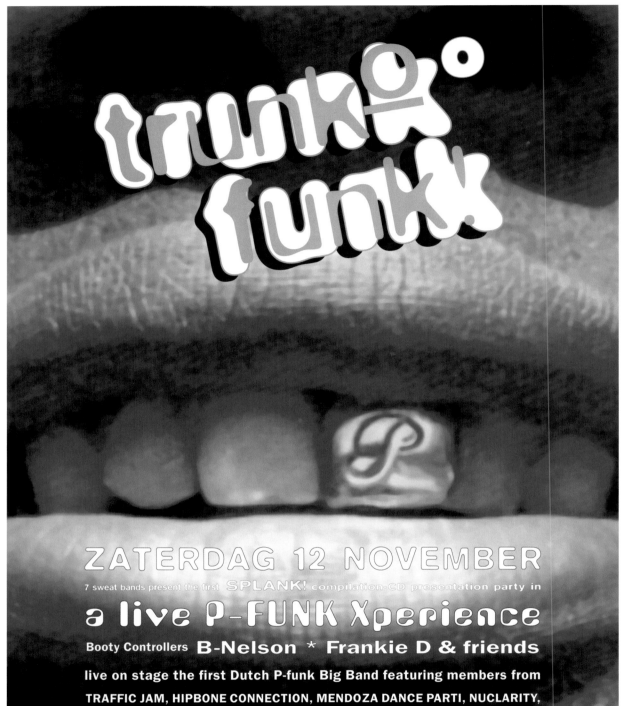

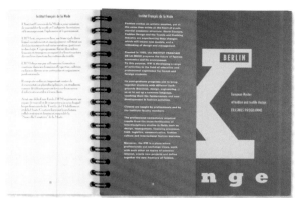

Barter as Design Criterion

Fifteen European fashion students at the Institut Français de la Mode had been given the assignment to make their graduation catalogue together. They disagreed about whether the format should be horizontal or vertical and asked Dietwee to take charge of the design and help them with the layout of their presentations.

Given their tight budget, the available funds had to be used sparingly and cleverly. The designers walked into the school with the maximum possible number of print sheets: 5 pieces measuring 70x100 cm, partitioned into squares of 10x10 cm. Each student was allotted 2 boxes per sheet. Only one sheet could be printed in full colour, and two sheets combined black with a supporting colour. The other two were to be in black and white.

By bartering with each other, the students could satisfy a preference for colour or totally black and white, and because the sheets were cut into different formats after being printed, they could even settle the horizontal or vertical dispute simply: everyone got the format that they wanted.

Dietwee translated a nearly impossible desire for diversity into a working procedure that offered flexibility and put part of the responsibility for the design back into the hands of the students themselves. It supplied the framework, preserved cohesion and elevated the principal of bartering to the title of the book.

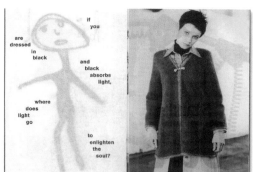

Inventive Minimalism

Don't tell beginning design labels in the Netherlands anything about start-up problems. Just when Dutch fashion design had begun to break out of what had seemed an eternal impasse, it lacked every facility to finance promising collections and put them on the market. Stigters was one such young label that wished to make a name for itself in the retail market, but absolutely did not have the necessary financial means. Inventiveness was the only expedient.

Like the idea of attaching to every piece of clothing a small catalogue (9x13 cm) that simultaneously served as a price tag. This format was still very unusual at the time, and the idea of using the price tag as a catalogue of products would familiarize every buyer – as well as the people in their immediate circles – with the quality of the entire collection. The graphic design had to achieve a maximal communicative effect while working under minimal condi-

tions. Just as with the Parisian fashion students, using printing paper as thriftily as possible was the starting point. Everything that could be printed on the same kind of paper was assembled on and cut from the same sheet; business cards, labels and catalogue covers were printed together, and the 70 gram half-transparent inner pages of the catalogues were printed side by side with letter and invoice paper.

BSO/ORIGIN ONDERNEMINGSRAAD

Whatever You Make, You End Up Getting More Back

Just how important distinctive (low-budget) commissions are for a start-up agency was clearly shown when software developer BSO/Origin got in touch with Dietwee. The company, scouting for new designers in the Utrecht area, had been handed a copy of the X-Change catalogue and on the strength of that approached Dietwee about designing the annual report of their works council. Shortly before, BSO and the Philips subsidiary Origin had merged. Two corporate cultures were to be united with each other, and the annual report would provide information about that. The members of the works council each wrote a section of the report, and the designers introduced the metaphor of bridges. Text and images (archive photographs from the Ministry of Transport) connected up in curious ways, strengthening the concept of the report. Although the booklet – bound in wire-o and composed of whole and half pages – was only printed in two colours, by washing the printing press frequently the designers were able to work with various colours of ink. The result is a colourful report that became the foundation of an intensive collaboration between BSO/Origin and Dietwee.

A Butterfly and a Heavyweight

A small wonder can be achieved within a few days. Even when the director torpedoes the first design on account of an incomplete briefing – because that can spark an important personal contact. When CEO Eckart Wintzen saw the proposal that the designers had made for the presentation of 'Rainbow', the new internal management program at BSO/Origin, he immediately decided to take over the supervision of his communications department, because otherwise there would be too little time to complete the project properly.

'Masterpiece' was supposed to bring the Rainbow program to the attention of the 5000 employees working at BSO/Origin worldwide. As a first introduction to the program, Dietwee chose a series of seven volumes of poetry, in which four poems by George Moorman were printed in 10 major languages including Chinese and Japanese. The butterfly images reflected the logo that Dietwee had designed for Rainbow: a butterfly with a rainbow projected on it. More important than the printed result was the expanded scale that Masterpiece brought into play. Suddenly the designers were sitting as equal partners at the same table as the heads of the company. The 1994 annual report would just be a matter of time.

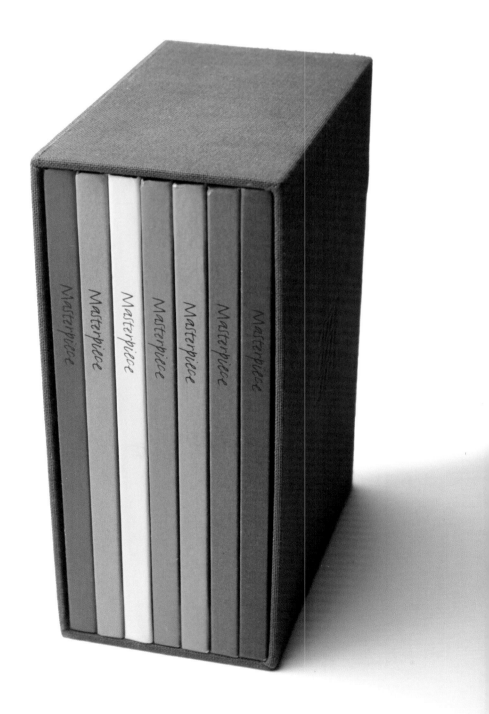

MASTERPIECE

Jeszcze tego samego wieczoru otrzymałem Twój list, w którym

opisałaś cud tego popołudnia - że

"iris" oznacza to samo, co "tęczówka".

That night I receive your letter
describing the miracle of this afternoon:
that Iris and iris are one.

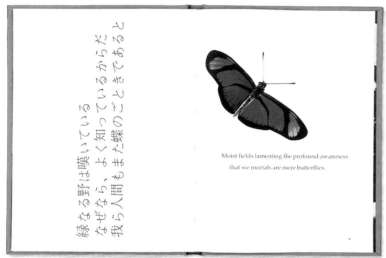

緑なる野は嘆いている
なぜなら、よく知っているからだ
我ら人間もまた蝶のごとくであると

Moist fields lamenting the profound awareness
that we mortals are mere butterflies.

THE MOMENT OF TRUTH

THE EYES OF IRIS

Bunu anlamam uzun sürdü
fakat şimdi
karşında
duruyorum
ve anlıyorum ki böylesine
özlü bir bakış
hiç de gölge gibi hafif
değil.

It has taken me long, but now that I am finally facing you
I realize that such a decisive
glance is far from shadow-like light.

Seven Minutes of Fame

The introductory note to 'Dossier 94', BSO/Origin's annual report, says enough: 'Here is your copy of Dossier 94. It contains more or less everything that was of importance for BSO/Origin during the past year: The company in action, as reported and photographed by employees around the world. The financial results and the effects upon the environment. Third-party commentary and views on today and tomorrow. In short, what went on last year can be found in the Dossier. Not a classical annual report, but complete, and characteristic of what concerns us.' The assignment, which came straight from the board of directors, was simple: Make sure that we can cap-ture the attention of Jan Timmer, the CEO of Philips, for seven minutes. A decision to avoid all glossiness and assemble a dossier of loose documents dove-tailed perfectly with the company's mindset of wanting to let its human side prevail over a display of financial muscle.

The initial idea of sending photographers who had recently won the Silver Camera out to roam across the world was quickly dropped. Instead, Dietwee dispatched disposable cameras and requested employees at all of the different branches to make portraits of themselves, their work and their clients. The material that was sent back – no matter where it had come from – proved to display such a high degree of similarity that the designers could limit themselves to a simple grouping of themes.

Turn a new tab page and you might find graphics or a global map showing all of the branches. Each time a new surprise awaited someone leafing through the material: newspaper photocopies, an account book with figures. Dossier 94 was an annual report in its purest form, a collection of anecdotes, clippings, charts, photos. What would normally have been the starting point of a design process had been made into the finished product.

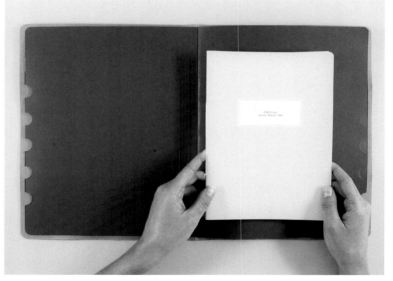

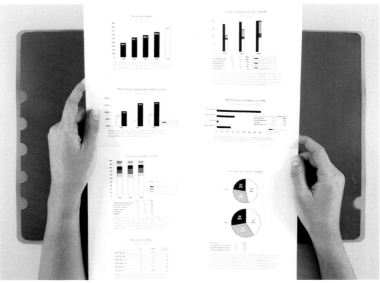

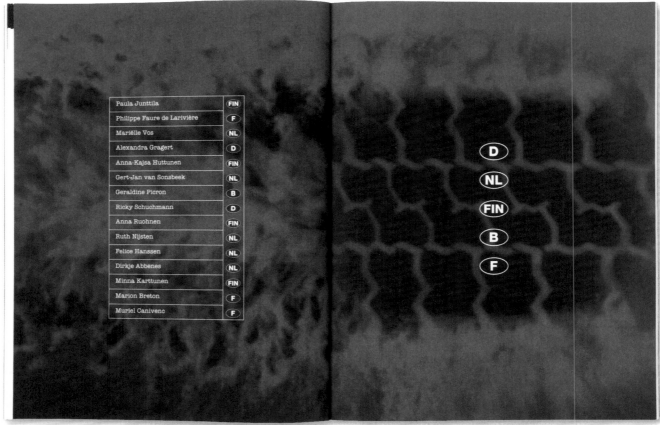

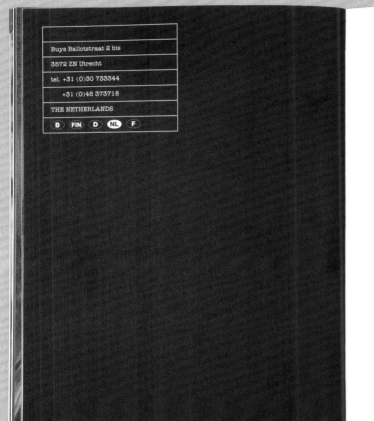

Buys Ballotstraat 2 bis

3572 ZN Utrecht

tel. +31 (0)30 733344

+31 (0)46 373718

THE NETHERLANDS

B FIN D NL F

purity of line

clarity of shape

"simplicity is the last refuge of the complicated mind"
(Oscar Wilde)

RIEN NE SE PERD

NOTHING IS LOST

RIEN NE SE CRÉE

NOTHING IS CREATED

TOUT SE TRANSFORME

EVERYTHING IS MOVING

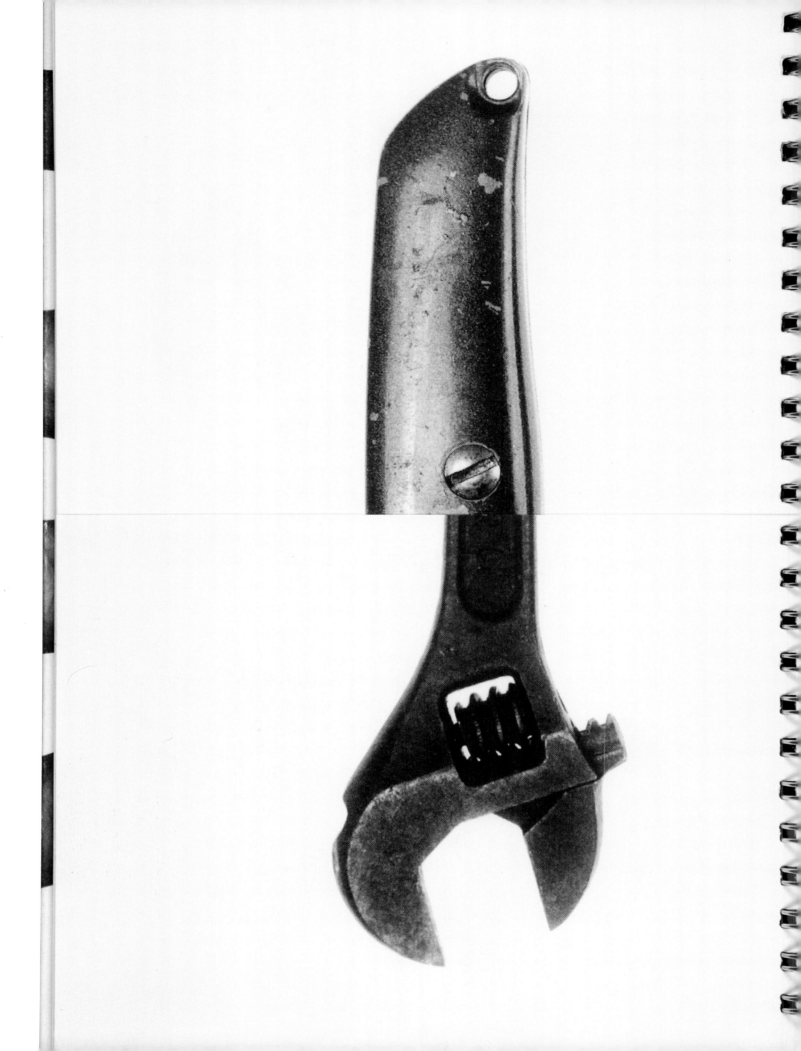

Confusing Decisiveness

The task of the BSO/Origin works council was no simple one. As the intermediary between employees and management, it had been made responsible for ensuring that the agreements made that year were carried out, but the link-up was far from perfect. Decisiveness was required. With that as theme, the designers made the second works council annual report, assisted by Richard van der Laken (who is now a partner of the Designpolitie). Just as with the 'bridges' booklet of the previous year, whole and half pages were used, only this time to purposely cover up parts of images and texts or let them flow from one into another. The theme was represented by tools, which mutated into strange new forms as the pages were turned. In this manner, the works council implied that they could be seen as a tool, but not just any tool.

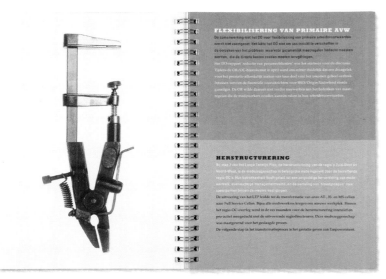

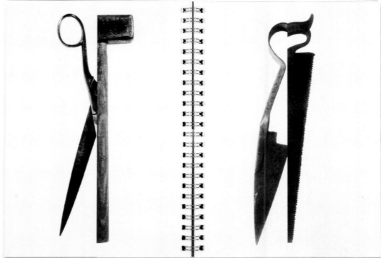

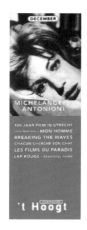

JANUARI

CINEMA KOREA

DE MAN MET DE HOND

HET VIJFDE SEIZOEN · MOVIEZONE

2 MINUTEN STILTE A.U.B.

HET FANTASTISCHE LUCHTSCHIP

CINEMA 2000 · WERELDCINEMA

SUNDAY JAZZ · LOLA RENNT

LITERAIR HUISKAMERONWEER

SUNDAY JAZZ · SLEEPING MAN

COMEDIAN HARMONISTS

ROTTERDAM FILM COURSE · AYNEH

HAMAM, IL BAGNO TURCO

FILMTHEATER
't Hoogt

BIN ICH SCHÖN?
doris dörrie

Bin ich Schön? gaat over de droom iemand anders te zijn. We volgen de met elkaar verbonden verhalen van vier stellen die op zoek zijn naar geluk en hun leven willen veranderen. Meer dan dertig acteurs werkten mee aan Bin ich Schön?. De opnames hadden dus wel wat voeten in de aarde.

VERWACHT IN JUNI

JACKY
fow zyng hu & brat lohft

Dit speelfilmdebuut van twee afgestudeerden aan de filmacademie, werd prompt geselecteerd voor een belangrijk bijprogramma van het Festival in Cannes. Jacky is een 25-jarige Chinese zoon van geëmigreerde ouders. Jacky vormt een portret van de Chinese gemeenschap in Nederland.

IL DECAMERON
pier paolo pasolini

Pier Paolo Pasolini (1922-1975) was een totaalkunstenaar die afwisselend de pen, de kwast en de camera hanteerde. Hij wordt in Italië beschouwd als de meest oorspronkelijke dichter van zijn generatie. In 1975 werd hij vermoord.

Pasolini verplaatste voor zijn film de handeling naar Napels en omstreken. De Napolitaanse spreektaal en liedjes vormen een van de vele charmes van de film.

Vanwege het vele mannelijk en vrouwelijk bloot zijn er sinds de première van Il Decameron ruim 150 aanklachten tegen de film ingediend!

Food for Freaks

With its arthouse cinema activities, Filmtheatre 't Hoogt targets the enthusiast. That group's appetite for information is enormous, and halfway through the nineties it could barely be satisfied through the digital media. So for Dietwee, a change of house style was more than just replacing the previous Memphis-like aura with a more sober image. Choosing Avenir as the body type in the monthly program bulletin and using a Din with a blurred effect in the logo certainly contributed to the increased commercialization, but more important was the structuring of information. Film descriptions were edited rigorously and typeset in such a way that they never ran on to the next page. Here the poetry was not in the presentation, but in the subtle reference of the logo to projected subtitles and most of all, in the mystery of the film stills, which were given a prominent place on the cover and in the interior of the two-colour bulletins.

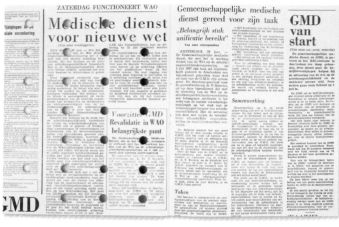

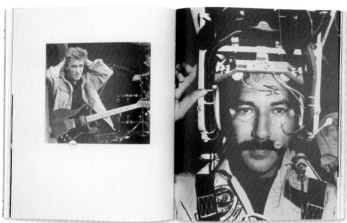

25 Years of Chasing After the Facts

After 25 years of implementing the disability law, the curtain fell for the Joint Medical Service (GMD). For a quarter of a century, the controversial GMD had screened people for disability compensation but also offered medical support to people who were wholly or partially incapacitated for work. Constant changes in the law, however, had continually introduced new complications in performing that task, and people at the GMD felt that they had been chasing after the facts right up to the very second it closed.

The jubilee year was commemorated, ironically enough, with a farewell book. The book opens with a flyleaf upon which are printed newspaper articles about the origins of the GMD; at its end, another flyleaf bears reports of its demise. In between them, two stories run parallel: a description of the actual career of the GMD and a second story (with illustrations) about social developments during that period. Dietwee did the visual research themselves, choosing photos of news items and events that immediately evoke associations for every Dutch person: the country's first and only astronaut; John Lennon and Yoko Ono in the Hilton hotel…. The cover refers back to the circulation-envelope and the 25 punch holes mark the place where each year is located in the interior. In this project, Faas and Francés worked closely with Annelies Dollekamp, Dietwee's first employee.

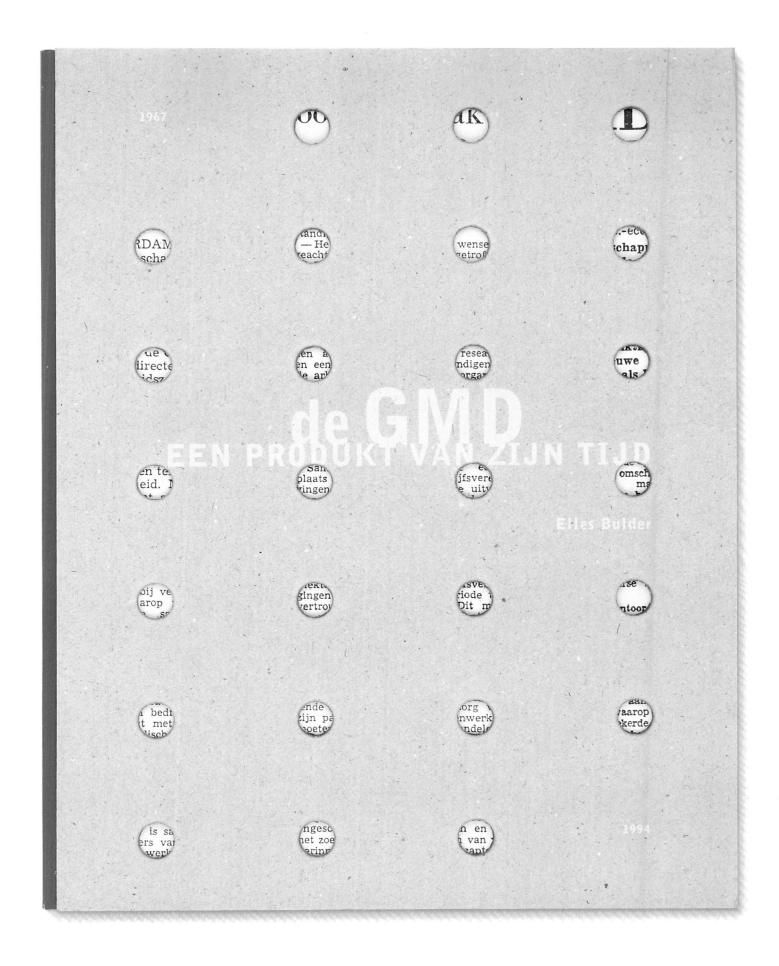

Party Fan

For the 1996/97 New Year's Eve, a party with 6 themes was organized in 6 different spaces of the 'Utrechtse School' (a 19th century building now serving as a theatre) by the Rebellenclub, a group of party professionals who came together every year for the New Year's celebrations simply because they wanted to throw a really great party – with quality, not commercial interest, as their only goal. Like a fan of coloured samples for paint, the invitations for the parties were bolted together at one corner by a plastic screw. Tickets to these parties always sold out within a few hours after presales were launched.

Dance or Die!

At first the flyers for BoomBoom were extremely typographic, but a growing emphasis on the funky image of these nights also brought about a change in the visual language. Space guns gave a new twist to the notion of BoomBoom: It was no longer the boom of the house-beat that was translated, but the crack of a pistol.

PARADISO - DONDERDAG 17 OKTOBER

BOOMBOOM! DE LUXE

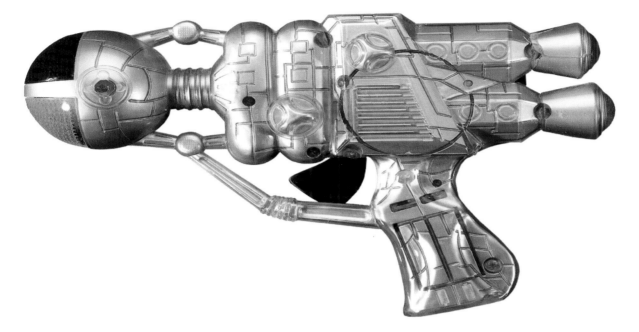

**MORCHEEBA - BABY FOX - LAMB
THE HORN (Jedi Knights) - FRETLESS AZM
DEEJAYS LX PACIFIC, FRANKIE D & TOM MIDDLETTON**
LEADERS OF THE NU-SKOOL - REHUMANISING THE ELECTRONIC TRADITION

BOOMBOOM! DE VILLE

ZATERDAG 21 SEPTEMBER
DEEJAYS LX PACIFIC & FRANKIE D
WE TAKE A LOOK AT - NOT JUST MUSIC - BUT SOUND ITSELF

BOOMBOOM! DE VILLE

ZATERDAG 23 NOVEMBER
DEEJAYS LX PACIFIC, FRANKIE D & FRIENDS
THE COUNTERWEIGHT DYNAMIC DANCE SOUND, GOOD VIBES UNCOMPROMISED

OR-verkiezingen

Mede in het kader van de professionalisering van de
medezeggenschap is continuïteit binnen de ondernemingsraad
een vereiste, te bereiken met veel herverkiesbare kandidaten.
Negen van de zeventien zittende leden gaven gehoor aan deze
wens en werden allen herkozen. De overige kandidaten
overigens ook van goed medezeggenschapskaliber, te w
drie leden uit vorige OR'en, drie recentelijke OC-leden.
Drie enthousiaste (vrouwelijke) nieuwelingen als aanwinst
maakten de club compleet.

Bite

A new merger brought together software developer BSO/Origin and Philips C&P. Greater competition in an increasingly aggressive market had necessitated this joining of forces, which demanded a willingness for cooperation and dedication from the corporation itself. 'Commitment' was accordingly the theme of the 1995 Social Annual Report.

The works council had two messages. One for the management, to make it clear that the agreements that had been made in relation to the merger with Philips could not be rescinded; and one for the employees, to get them to participate in the efforts of the works council. Both parties were asked for commitment – suggested straight away on the cover by a pit bull who bites into a stick and will

not let go. Throughout the report are photographs representing the will for cooperation and survival. The Japanese binding method hides a good portion of the actual contents. Only those who are interested and willing enough to tear open the uncut pages will get the entire story. People who received the report were notified by e-mail a few days later that if the pages hadn't been torn open by then, they clearly lacked interest and commitment.

Although this was a fully 'corporate' assignment, Dietwee used the playfulness with which it had experimented repeatedly to stir up interest with its designs for flyers. Once curiosity was aroused, commitment would increase. That formula both worked in the party scene and the corporate world.

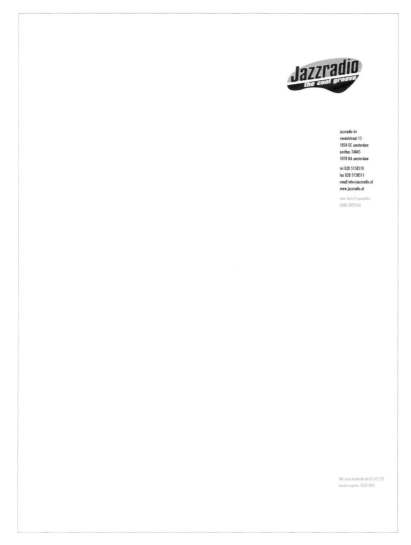

Blue Note Nineties

When Jazzradio started up in Holland, target-group
radio was a fairly unknown phenomenon.
Director Stanja van Mierlo wanted its house style
to depict a clearer image of the broad interpretation
people give to jazz: a melting pot of jazz, rhythm &
blues, soul and funk. The design referred, indeed,
to the classic Blue Note albums – where the roots
of Jazzradio lay – but ushered that style into the
nineties through colour and form.

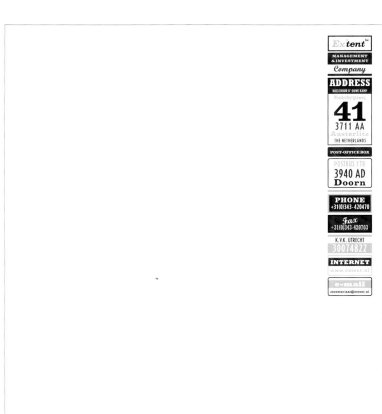

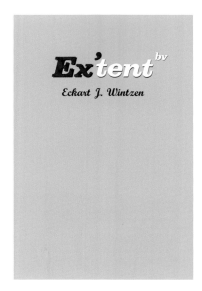

Eck's place

Twenty years after he had founded BSO and saw it grow to more than 10.000 people worldwide, Eckart Wintzen said goodbye to his software company. With management and investment company Ex'tent, he wanted to return to small entrepreneurship. Ex'tent would only invest and participate in companies making a real contribution to society: green capital funds, but also the American ice cream brand Ben and Jerry's, which he introduced to the Netherlands because of that company's social involvement. The house style of Ex'tent would be a homage to small business. In the booklet 'Yes, we're open', owners pose in front of the doors of their establishments: Jan's place; Henk's place. The design of the letter paper refers to the credit card stickers and other signs on neighbourhood store windows.

Serious Play

Particularly because of the recognition brought to them by the reports for
BSO/Origin, Dietwee rapidly gained the reputation of a design agency that had
arrived. The truth was otherwise, both in terms of finances and commissions.
So when the commission from consulting agency Quadrant Communication came,
it was a real godsend. Quadrant, specialized in interactive educational information
and training, was looking for a house style that would express in a simple manner
the playfulness and creativity which differentiated them from others in a heavily
competitive market. Simulated flying for pilots, training courses for ambulance
personnel and train conductors: in each case, the interactive communication involved the use of eye, hand, ear, and voice. These four elements formed the basis
for a design that revived the concept of the chance encounters of different images
in the BSO tool booklet. With whole and half pages, impossible, surreal combinations of images occur.

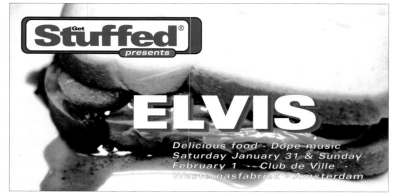

Branded Stuff

Dancing is only dancing, after all. 'Get Stuffed' ordered up a new formula for a complete night out: a wine, dine & dance experience, each time featuring a new theatrical theme provided by the Ready Maids and Arne Koefoed of Wink Party Artwork. Every month in Amsterdam's Westergasfabriek they created a totally different experience. Strange but exotic food, unexpected acts and bizarre decorations were the overture to a spectacular dance feast. Flyers promoted Get Stuffed, and soon the event itself worked as a brand name.

Incent(ive)

Better a good rip-off than a bad design. Only a Chinese visitor to the New Year's Party in the Winkel van Sinkel would have read about a dragon's being literally ripped off a package of incense. Add the appropriate typography and yet another invitation could go out the door.

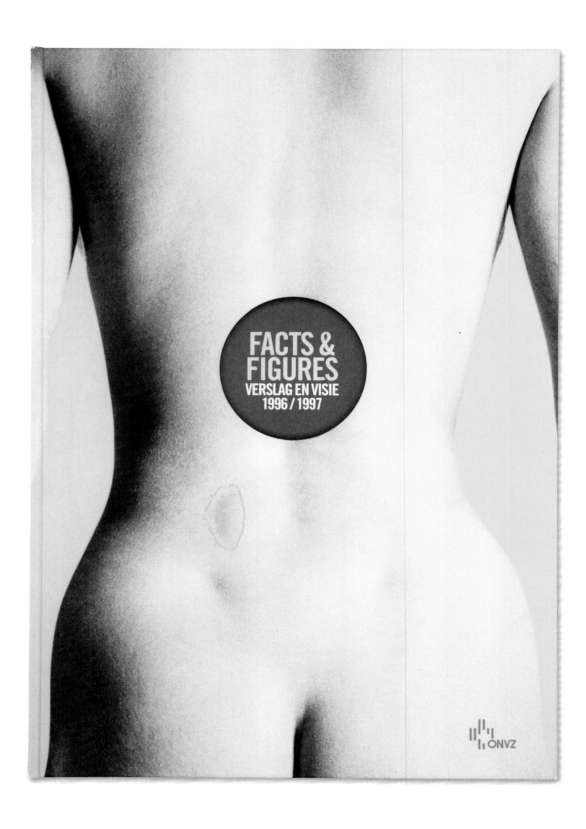

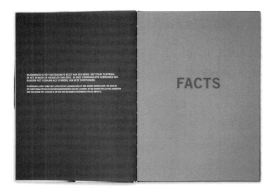
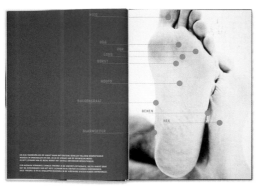

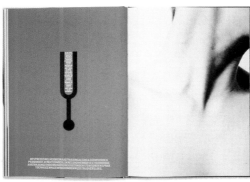

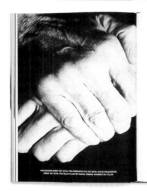

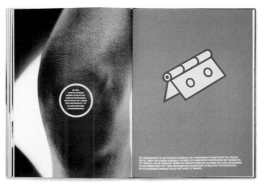
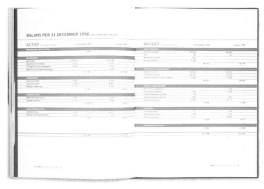

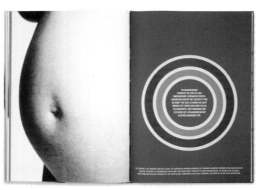

Body Talk

Some clients are personally important when it comes to achieving a good result. Like Arne Koefoed for Hardbop and later Wink and Eckart Wintzen for BSO/Origin, director Frans van Rijn of health insurer ONVZ was ideal to brainstorm with. His ambition of giving ONVZ a high-quality market profile clicked at once with the creative ambitions of the young agency. The slogan 'You insure your most precious possession with ONVZ' had been set when Dietwee was asked if they could think up something around it for an annual report. The answer was affirmative and the designers started looking for all sorts of interesting facts about the human body. What is the relationship between dizziness and the ear? On an average human head, 11 kilometres of hair grows in one year. There is enough glycerine in the body to produce 15 kilos of explosives. And just exactly where on the tongue are the taste buds? In short: What is that precious possession, in fact?

For Facts & Figures, Dietwee worked with graphic designer SYB and photographer Frans Jansen.

SPIEREN ZIJN NIET RECHTSTREEKS VERBONDEN MET DE BOTTEN. AAN HET EINDE VAN DE SPIER ZIT EEN STUKJE PEES. DEZE PEES IS AAN HET BOT GEHECHT EN BRENGT DE TREKKRACHT VAN DE SPIER OVER NAAR HET BOT. DE BEKENDSTE PEES IS DE PEES VAN ACHILLES. AL VOOR ZIJN GEBOORTE WAS VOORSPELD DAT ACHILLES, DE ZOON VAN THETIS, ZIJN VADER NAAR DE KROON ZOU STEKEN. DAAROM DORST NOCH ZEUS, DE KONING DER GODEN, NOCH ZIJN BROER POSEIDON, DE MOOIE THETIS HET HOF TE MAKEN. DE GODEN HUWELIJKTEN HAAR UIT AAN EEN STERFELIJKE HEERSER. THETIS PROBEERDE IETS TE DOEN AAN DE STERFELIJKHEID VAN HAAR ZOON ACHILLES. HOMERUS VERTELT DAT ZIJ HAAR KIND DAARTOE IN DE STYX, DE RIVIER VAN HADES, ONDERDOMPELDE. OMDAT ZE HEM NIET LOS KON LATEN ZONDER DAT ACHILLES ZOU VERDRINKEN, HIELD ZE HEM BIJ ZIJN HIEL VAST. HET WATER VAN DE STYX DAT HEM ONSTERFELIJK MAAKTE BEREIKTE HEM DAAR DUS NIET. ZIJN HIEL BLEEF DAARDOOR DE ENIGE KWETSBARE PLEK VAN ZIJN LICHAAM. OMDAT ZIJ WIST DAT ACHILLES VOORBESTEMD WAS OM IN TROJE TE SNEUVELEN, DEED THETIS ALLES OM TE VERMIJDEN DAT HIJ ZICH IN DE KRIJGSKUNST ZOU BEKWAMEN. TOCH KON ZIJ NIET VOORKOMEN DAT HIJ VERMAARD WERD OM ZIJN GROTE VAARDIGHEID IN HET GEVECHT. DAT WAS VOOR ODYSSEUS AANLEIDING OM HEM BIJ AGEMEMNON, DE LEIDER VAN DE GRIEKSE EXPEDITIE TEGEN TROJE, TE INTRODUCEREN. ACHILLES OVERLEEFDE VELE AVONTUREN EN GEVECHTEN. UITEINDELIJK WERD HIJ GEDOOD DOOR EEN GIFTIGE PIJL VAN PARIS, DIE, GELEID DOOR DE ZONNEGOD APOLLO, PRECIES ZIJN KWETSBARE HIEL RAAKTE.

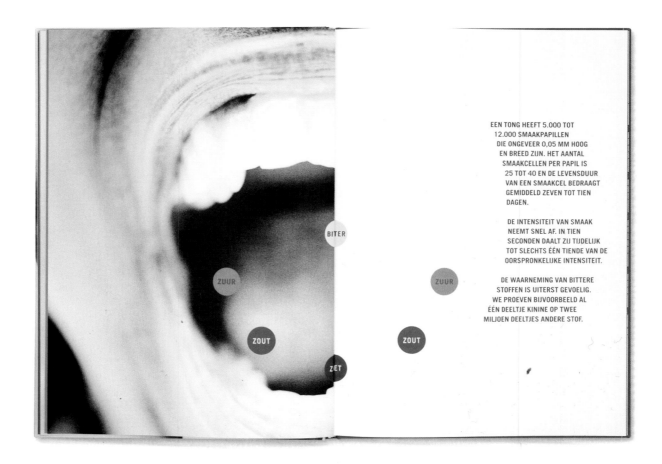

EEN TONG HEEFT 5.000 TOT 12.000 SMAAKPAPILLEN DIE ONGEVEER 0,05 MM HOOG EN BREED ZIJN. HET AANTAL SMAAKCELLEN PER PAPIL IS 25 TOT 40 EN DE LEVENSDUUR VAN EEN SMAAKCEL BEDRAAGT GEMIDDELD ZEVEN TOT TIEN DAGEN.

DE INTENSITEIT VAN SMAAK NEEMT SNEL AF. IN TIEN SECONDEN DAALT ZIJ TIJDELIJK TOT SLECHTS ÉÉN TIENDE VAN DE OORSPRONKELIJKE INTENSITEIT.

DE WAARNEMING VAN BITTERE STOFFEN IS UITERST GEVOELIG. WE PROEVEN BIJVOORBEELD AL ÉÉN DEELTJE KININE OP TWEE MILJOEN DEELTJES ANDERE STOF.

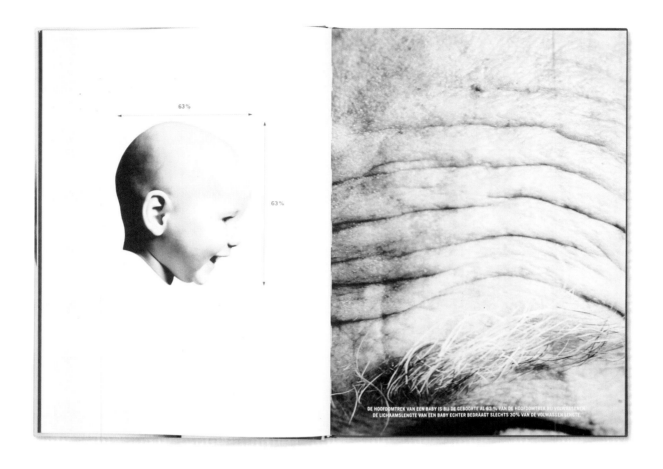

63%

63%

DE HOOFDOMTREK VAN EEN BABY IS BIJ DE GEBOORTE AL 63 % VAN DE HOOFDOMTREK BIJ VOLWASSENEN.
DE LICHAAMSLENGTE VAN EEN BABY ECHTER BEDRAAGT SLECHTS 30% VAN DE VOLWASSEN LENGTE.

11 KM

HAAR GROEIT BIJ ELKAAR GEMIDDELD 11 KM PER JAAR:
ONGEVEER DE AFSTAND VAN UTRECHT NAAR HOUTEN.

NIET ALLE MENSEN HEBBEN EVENVEEL HAAR. AZIATISCHE MENSEN HEBBEN HET MEESTE HOOFDHAAR:
ONGEVEER 120.000 HAREN. AFRIKAANSE MENSEN ONGEVEER 110.000, BLONDE MENSEN 100.000, ROODHARIGEN 80.000.
VROUWEN HEBBEN GEMIDDELD MEER HOOFDHAAR DAN MANNEN.

Problem Solving / Opportunity Seeking

The Drum Rhythm Festival was one of the tobacco industry's answers to the ban on cigarette advertizing. By creating a large music festival, Drum could reach a young target group. However, publicity was not easy. The diversity of styles on the program (Hip Hop, Jungle and Breakbeats alongside world music) made it very difficult to determine one specific image for the festival. There was a theme poster to announce the event, and concert organizer Mojo produced separate posters with the names of the artists. Advertising agency FHV-BBDO had been struggling with the poster for some time. Creative minds kept concocting new solutions, but two weeks before the deadline they still hadn't hit the right note. Dietwee, who previously had made a flyer for Drum Rhythm, were called in to help; amongst the copy the designers spied the phrase 'Get Mixed Up'. They suggested that the festival should fly under that flag. They agreed with Mojo that the separate posters would be included in the overall design so as to spread one coherent image, typographically set in the house colours of the sponsor: red and blue. Simple, and on time.

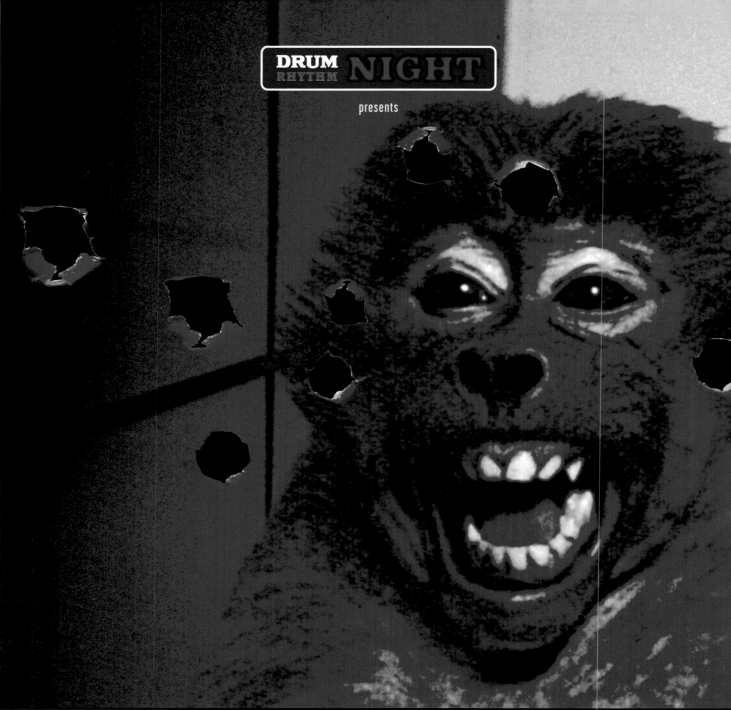

DRUM RHYTHM NIGHT

presents

"...Monkey Mafia is for tomorrow's dancefloor; most likely to scare your mum..." (Mixmag) | **DJ SET** | **Hard Hands** | **UK**

MONKEY MAFIA

Pressure Drop

Tuesday June 30 - EFFENAAR - Eindhoven Supporting dj Loes Lee   Doors open at 21:00 Admission ƒ12,50

Wednesday July 1 - NIGHTTOWN THEATER - Rotterdam Supporting dj's Flipjack & Loes Lee
Doors open at 22.00 Admission ƒ12,50

Thursday July 2 - PAARD - Den Haag Supporting dj Eric Denz Da Denz   Doors open at 22.00 Admission ƒ15,-

Friday July 3 CLUB DE VILLE - Westergasfabriek - Amsterdam Supporting dj LX Pacific
Doors open at 23.00 Admission ƒ12,50

EFFENAAR (PHONE 040-2448861)   NIGHTTOWN (PHONE 010-4363534)   PAARD (PHONE 070-3601838)   CLUB DE VILLE (PHONE 020-5974458)

design. alf@dietwee.nl printed by Reijt

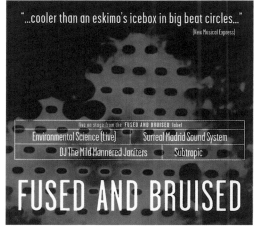

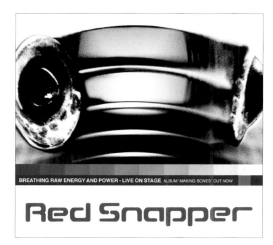

Who Shot the Monkey?

In addition to the festival, cigarette manufacturer Drum also sponsored a series
of Drum Rhythm Nights. These were on a smaller scale and more daring than
the large festival, exclusively giving attention to promising acts in the international
dance scene that had not yet had a breakthrough. With the Nights, in contrast
to the festival, its focused program made working with images easily possible.
Dietwee took great liberty in interpreting names of bands and music styles, so that
it was obvious that the Nights were not album tours for the bands. But because
the posters were consistently printed in blue and red, the Nights clearly had a
characteristic signature. The sponsor's logo was presented with fitting restraint.

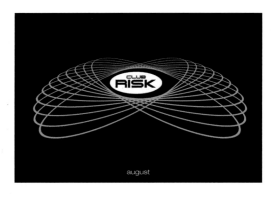

august

december

october

House and Style

Club Risk initially programmed the Friday nights in
the Winkel van Sinkel (a grand café cum restaurant/
dance club in Utrecht). Their dance events with top
DJs from the Netherlands, London and Chicago
brought a large audience in contact with House, but
growing competition had been continually reducing
the number of visitors. Although at first both Club Risk
and the Winkel van Sinkel were not completely con-
vinced of Dietwee's ability to make flyers and posters
that were specifically House, they decided to try it for
a half year, anyway. The previous work for somewhat
smaller-scale parties with different sorts of music such
as Hard Bop and BoomBoom and for Drum Rhythm
had apparently all yielded its fruit. Dietwee decided
that a more stylish, subdued approach would boost
the popularity of the nights, and that Club Risk should
be treated more like a commercial brand. They up-
dated the logo. Like many others, the designers
searched for a way of graphically translating the beat
of House, and found it in the Spirograph box.

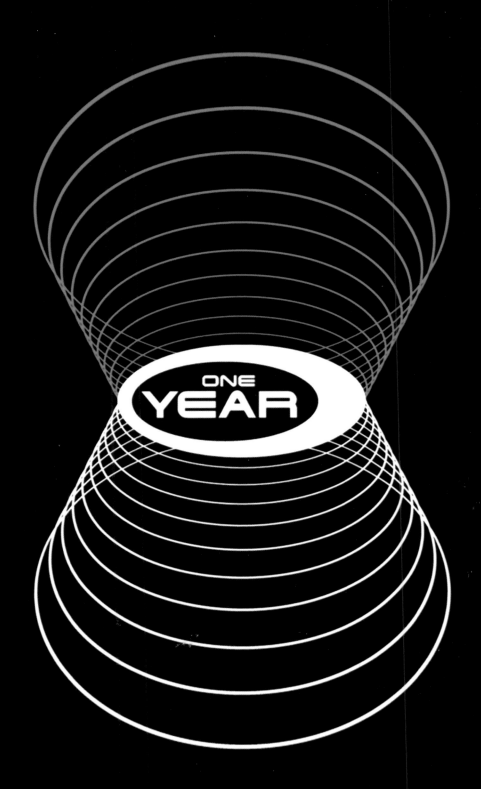

Club Risk One Year Anniversary

September 11 Westbam (Lowsprit Rec., Berlin)

Angelo, Dimitri & Eric de Man

Downstairs: Garage by Jeppe & Timst'r

Special performance: Knee High Puppeteers with the Android Sisters

• • • special afterparty at Arena (Axl) with Angelo, Eric de Man & Richard • • •

September 4 Eric de Man & Michel de Hey
Downstairs: Big Beats by DJ Carlos

September 18 Remy & Angelo
Downstairs: Drum 'n Bass by DJ Jair

September 25 "U.S. Garage Night"
Live: ROSE (SOAP), Jeppe & Eric de Man
in cooperation with het Nederlands Film Festival

Winkel van Sinkel - Oudegracht 158 Utrecht
(ingang a/d werf) open 00.00-06.00 hrs
admission anniversary ƒ 25,- no presale

[aem´kei]   Design by Dylan & Tirso @ Dietwee

Work in Progress

No sooner had Yellowstone been set up than the ICT company instantly needed a house style in order to be able to sell its various types of service: network management, computerization, service contracts. Work, in short, that is never-ending. The phrase Under Construction was introduced in order to create a temporary house style. Not only was this concept applicable to a start-up company, but it also seemed relevant for the ICT sector, which, like roadwork, is subject to perpetual restructuring. As so often is the case, the temporary solution proved to be definitive. Under Construction was there to stay.

The Saloon

Six years ago, the Moira gallery organized a small
exhibition entitled The Saloon. It was the gallery's
answer to the Utrecht Salon, a tri-annual exhibition of
artists and designers in the city's Centraal Museum
which attempts to give a broad overview of present-
day art in Utrecht. De Moira had countered with her
own view of Utrecht's art by giving the artists in her
network an opportunity to exhibit.

Now, on the occasion of the third Salon, Moira again
organized The Saloon. Dietwee was commissioned
to make a poster, booklet and flyer for the event.
The idea was to produce everything at the lowest
possible price. They consequently decided to make
the booklet from the same material used for the flyer
and poster. Two flyers next to each other made the
cover, and for the inside, text was printed on the back
of the poster. Once folded into a quire, the cut-up
image of the poster resulted in chance images that
alternated with the pages of text.

Night Shopping

The Winkel van Sinkel was originally the first depart-ment store in the Netherlands. Since 1996 this impressive building in the centre of Utrecht has served as a café/restaurant and a dance club under the guidance of creative director Didier Prince. For two years, Saturday nights in the Winkel van Sinkel had been in the theme of The Big Mix, cross-over nights of funk, soul, breakbeats, hiphop, triphop and house music. At the time, there were many full-

colour flyers out-shouting each other for such kinds of events. Dietwee thought up a new concept: the Nachtwinkel (Night Shop), with a shopping cart as logo, an unchanging black background and typo-graphy that was always the same. The images on the flyers and the website refer to supermarkets but also relate to the theme of a particular night. For the 'Garden of Eden', for instance, this was a moist apple and a greased banana. Gradually, the concept of the

Nachtwinkel was developed further. Visitors were kept informed through monthly mailing lists and e-flyers of the latest 'special offers'; regular guests received a customer pass that was also good at other stores and every once in a while on Saturday nights the shopping cart – which made the website unsafe at unexpected moments – literally rode across the dance floor bringing the visitors snacks or little presents.

DE NACHTWINKEL >> APRIL/MEI 1999
EEN NIEUWE LENTE EN EEN NIEUW GELUID

DE NACHTWINKEL >> JUNI/JULI 1999
UTRECHT S GROOTSTE BLIJFT OP DE KLEINTJES LETTEN

DE NACHTWINKEL >> JULI/AUG 1998
MAAK HIER UW KEUZE

DE NACHTWINKEL >> SEPT/OKT 1998
OP ZATERDAG BIEDT UW WARENHUIS EEN PROGRESSIEF DANSASSORTIMENT
GEPRESENTEERD DOOR DE NIEUWE FILIAALCHEF MIKE E

UW VRUCHTEN >> PLUK NU UW VRUCHTEN >> PLUK NU UW

DATUM	PARTERRE	SOUTERRAIN
ZAT. 14 NOV.	**DE TUIN DER LUSTEN 1** (GULA – DE GULZIGHEID) LIVE VIDEO & MUSIC HECTIC ILUSIONS JET-SET > DEEJAYS OLLIE & PETI	THE MOVIEROOM (GULZIGE FILMS)
ZAT. 10 OKT.	JFK PRESENTEERT CASSIE 6 & MAESTRO	MARTINEZ (TECHNO/TRANCE)
ZAT. 17 OKT.	HEINEKEN CROSSOVER AWARDS B&B SOUND SYSTEM > BASCO > U GENE & OH JAY > ENERGIZER: FLIPJACK & PARADIZE (BONOBO)	RED (DELICIOUS)
ZAT. 24 OKT.	EASY ALOHA'S	D.JOOST (PROGRACID)
ZAT. 31 OKT.	CLUB RISK PRESENTEERT SUPERSONIC MET K.C. THE FUNKAHOLIC, FRANKIE D & THE 010 B BOYS	CLUB RISK SOUNDSYSTEM
ZAT. 7 NOV.	TESTLAB MET EDDY DE CLERCQ SPECIAL GUEST: CUT & PASTE (FRESKANOVA U.K.) AROMATHERAPIE / MASSAGE GENEROUSLY SPONSORED BY CHI	BOB (GOA/TRANCE)

>> LET OP - INTRODUCEEKAARTEN VERKRIJGBAAR TUSSEN 24.00 EN 02.00 UUR BIJ MIKE E <<

WINKEL VAN SINKEL, OUDEGRACHT 158, UTRECHT, INGANG AAN DE WERF. AANVANG 24.00 UUR. TOEGANG FL 12,50.
LEDEN EN INTRODUCÉES HEBBEN VOORRANG AAN DE DEUR.

DE NACHTWINKEL >> OKT/NOV 1998
OP ZATERDAG BIEDT UW WARENHUIS EEN ZINNEPRIKKELEND ELEND EN VOORUITSTREVEND
DANSASSORTIMENT VAN EERSTE KLAS EXPORTKWALITEIT

DE NACHTWINKEL >> SEPT/OKT 1999
LAAT JE INPAKKEN!

DE NACHTWINKEL >> MEI/JUNI 1999
DROP IT

DE NACHTWINKEL >> JUL/AUG 1999
ONZE DANSVLOEREN ZIJN VOLLEDIG GEAUTOMATISEERD

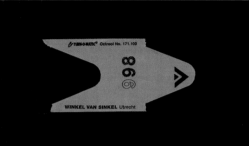

DE NACHTWINKEL >> NOV/DEC 1998
PRIKKELEND, RIJP EN VOORUITSTREVEND: MIKE E. PRESENTEERT
EEN DANSASSORTIMENT VAN FORMAAT

DE NACHTWINKEL >> FEB/MRT 1999
BINNENKORT: VOOR, TIJDENS OF NA HET DANSEN
NACHTDINEREN IN UW WARENHUIS. KEUKEN OPEN TOT 04.00 UUR

LEKKERSTE ZELF >> SCAN HET LEKKERSTE ZELF >> SCAN HET

DATUM	PARTERRE	SOUTERRAIN
ZAT.28.AUG.	**EDDY DE CLERCQS TESTLAB** SOLO PERFORMANCE BY E.D.C. & AROMATHERAPIE DOOR VALENTINE	BOB (GOA)
ZAT.31.JUL.	SUPERSONIC MET KC THE FUNKAHOLIC & FRANKIE D	RISK SOUNDSYSTEM
ZAT.07.AUG.	FUNKY NU SKOOL BREAKS PARTY MET FREQ. NASTY. (U.K.), SVENDEX & MIKE E, CHAMELIAN (SUB)	SIXX & ALPHA (TECH/TRANCE)
ZAT.14.AUG.	U-DANCE RADARS MUSIC MAGIC INTRODUCING MAGIC PRUT (A PSYKO SUMMER DISCOFIESTA)	D.JOOST (PROGRACID)
ZAT.21.AUG.	NACHTWINKEL SUMMERDISCO MET RONNY HAMMOND & ALWIN (METRO)	MAU (NIGHTFLIGHT)

>> LET OP - INTRODUCEEKAARTEN VERKRIJGBAAR BIJ UW HOST MIKE E <<

WINKEL VAN SINKEL, OUDEGRACHT 158, UTRECHT, INGANG AAN DE WERF. AANVANG 24.00 UUR. ENTREE FL.15,00.
LEDEN EN INTRODUCÉES HEBBEN VOORRANG AAN DE DEUR. INFO: WWW.DEWINKELVANSINKEL.NL WWW.BACARDI.COM

NIEUW ASSORTIMENT >> LET OP! BINNENKORT NIEUW ASSORTIMENT >> LET OP!

DATUM	PARTERRE	SOUTERRAIN
ZAT.09.OKT.	**AUTUMN DISCO** ALWIN (METRO), RONNY HAMMOND (DEDICATED MOTHERFUCKER) & DEEJAY PRUT (MAGIC)	D.JOOST (PROGRACID)
ZAT.04.SEPT.	HEPCAT'S FRUIT4EARS PRESENTS BIG-BEAT-CIRCUS MET ELECTRIC LADY AIDA	RISK SOUNDSYSTEM: DJ CMC & THE LOVEMACHINE ON 4 DECKS !
ZAT.11.SEPT.	STEPS 'N BREAKS BY LOES LEE (BITCHVILLE) & MIKE E	BOB (GOA)
ZAT.18.SEPT.	TRY-ANGLE '99 FLIPSIDE, ALWIN AND LOTS OF OTHER DYNAMICS (CHECK DA SPECIAL FLYER)	SPECIAL
ZAT.25.SEPT.	NEDERLANDS FILM FESTIVAL INFO IN DE FESTIVAL-KRANT	DISCO
ZAT.02.OKT.	SUPERSONIC MET KC THE FUNKAHOLIC & FRANKIE D	RISK SOUNDSYSTEM: DJ CMC & THE LOVEMACHINE

>> LET OP – INTRODUCEEKAARTEN VERKRIJGBAAR BIJ UW HOST MIKE E <<

WINKEL VAN SINKEL, OUDEGRACHT 158, UTRECHT, INGANG AAN DE WERF. AANVANG 24.00 UUR. ENTREE FL.15,00.
LEDEN EN INTRODUCÉES HEBBEN VOORRANG AAN DE DEUR. INFO: WWW.DEWINKELVANSINKEL.NL WWW.BACARDI.COM

DE NACHTWINKEL >> JAN/FEB 1999
BINNENKORT: VOOR, TIJDENS OF NA HET DANSEN
NACHTDINEREN IN UW WARENHUIS. KEUKEN OPEN TOT 04.00

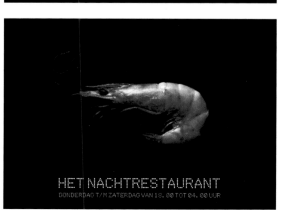

HET NACHTRESTAURANT
DONDERDAG T/M ZATERDAG VAN 18.00 TOT 04.00 UUR

Saturday October 31 - De Nachtwinkel

CLUB RISK IS READY TO TAKE YOU THROUGH THE SOUND BARRIER

K.C. THE FUNKAHOLIC (PARADISCO, BASSLINE)

FRANKY D. 010 B-BOYS FEATURING DJ CUT NICE

THE RISK SOUNDSYSTEM

FLY SUPERSONIC. FLY CLUB RISK. DEPARTURE > SAT. OCT. 31, 00.00 HRS. ARRIVAL > SUN. NOV. 1, 05.00 HRS.
WINKEL VAN SINKEL. INGANG AAN DE WERF. OUDE GRACHT 158. UTRECHT. TOEGANG FL 12,50
ONTWERP > ULEMAN@DIETWEE.NL

Saturday June 12

⊃ 22.00 HRS. ⊃ 05.00 HRS. ⊃ PARADISO ⊃ AMSTERDAM

Saturday February 13

⊃ 22.00 HRS. ⊃ 05.00 HRS. ⊃ PARADISO ⊃ AMSTERDAM

WE'RE BACK! ⊃ SATURDAY SEPTEMBER 19 1998 ⊃ 22.00 HRS - 05.00 HRS. ⊃ PARADISO

Saturday December 26

22.00 HRS. ⊃ 05.00 HRS. PARADISO ⊃ WELCOME TO THE FUTURE'S 5TH ANNIVERSARY

MAIN HALL ⊃ house, techno and more
Derrick May (Detroit, USA), Angelo and Eric de Man

THE MILLENIUM LOUNGE ⊃ fin de siècle mix
Zki presents Momono

IN TRANSIT ⊃ house classix
dj Basz and dj Babydoll

presale • limited tickets available • aub • de postkantoren • nieuwe muziekhandel, amsterdam • outland records, amsterdam • club wearhouse, amsterdam • twist and shout, utrecht • cyber records, leiden • g-sus, arnhem • paradiso, amsterdam • price: hfl.30,- excluding paradiso membership and presale fee door price: hfl.30,- excluding paradiso membership • paradiso, weteringschans 6-8, amsterdam • next future take off: saturday february 13, 1999 lights by gert hoek • design by uleman@dietwee.nl • decor by sis josip • a club risk / welcome to the future production

MAIN HALL ⊃ house, techno and more
Westbam (Losoul, Berlin), Angelo and Eric de Man

THE GARAGE LOUNGE ⊃ underground garage
Roog and Timst'r

IN TRANSIT ⊃ house classix
dj Basz and dj Babydoll

presale • limited tickets available • aub • de postkantoren • nieuwe muziekhandel, amsterdam • outland records, amsterdam • club wearhouse, amsterdam • twist and shout, utrecht • cyber records, leiden • g-sus, arnhem • paradiso, amsterdam • price: hfl.25,- excluding paradiso membership and presale fee • door price: hfl.30,- excluding paradiso membership • paradiso, weteringschans 6-8, amsterdam lights by gert hoek • design by uleman@dietwee.nl • decor by sis josip • a club risk / welcome to the future production

MAIN HALL ⊃ CD-PRESENTATION: DE NEDERLANDSCHE UNDERGROUND PART II

Airline Aesthetics

One of a series of posters for a once-every-six-weeks club night in the Winkel van Sinkel featuring a crossover between disco and big-beats. Retro seventies airlines and airports were the reference for the club decorations, hence the design.

The Future NOW

Flyers for a series of techno-house parties in Paradiso (Amsterdam), organized by Gert van Veen of Quazar and Club Risk. The pixelated image of the waterfall referred to how people might have to experience nature in the future: on a screen.

OPKOMST

ONGERENFESTIVAL

SCONCERTENTENTOONSTELLINGENPERFORMANCESVOORSTELLINGENCLINICS

2 T/M 26 OKTOBER UTRECHT

RMATIE OF RESERVEREN: 030 2332328

VST 1998 WORDT MEDE MOGELIJK GEMAAKT DOOR VSB FONDS, CJP PRINS BERNHARD FONDS,
UR DE PODIUMKUNSTEN, FONDS VOOR DE AMATEURKUNSTEN, TIVOLI, STADSSCHOUWBURG, BLAUWE ZAAL

CJP

VSB FONDS

In Full Flight

Youth festivals like De Opkomst (Up & Coming) are constantly searching for a new 'language' that can mobilize high school students to attend cultural events. A difficult target group – and most certainly when they themselves are central figures in the programming. With its work for the nightlife scene, Dietwee had by now proven that it spoke a language that might indeed come close to the one that these festivals were looking for. Over the years, De Opkomst and Dietwee created a series of posters, flyers and brochures that made a name for the program of the festival. De Opkomst organized theatre productions, shows and set up clinics in which, for instance, young talents were given the chance to scratch for an audience under the guidance of experienced DJs. The image of approaching seagulls was introduced by Harmen Liemburg, one of the subsequent founders of the Amsterdam design agency GM.

Desolate Beat

Super-low-budget flyer for the Progracid party in a squatted bunker in a desolate part of Amsterdam south. Noise represented as noise, in an aesthetic that seemingly effortlessly matched with the unrelentingly hard rhythms of the music and the desolate surroundings in which the party took place. There was actually no money at all, so the flyer was printed in one colour, but at least it was a metallic one.

Love from Granny

Every year the Summer Postage Stamp Foundation asks a different designer to design a stamp with a theme connected to the senior citizens. This year they clearly wanted the stamp to appeal more to a much younger public, and so the foundation and the Dutch PTT postal service asked Dietwee to come up with a concept for three stamps with the theme 'caring'.

Designing a senior citizens' stamp proved to be an enormous challenge due to the complexity of the subject. The stamps have a three-fold purpose. They are ordinary postage stamps, represent the theme of the foundation's annual campaign, and are a means of generating money for the foundation to finance its projects. Above all, the stamps had to be cheerful, clear, and striking.

Dietwee portrayed three types of care – caring about seniors, caring for seniors and seniors' caring for others – by actions everyone easily can recognize: relinquishing your seat to seniors, carrying groceries for your neighbor who can't walk well and getting a candy from Grandma. Senior citizens' care starts with the little things.

VPRO's moondive

MUSICIANS ON A MISSION
VRIJDAG 17 JULI PARADISO

AFLEVERING 2 **AANVANG 21.00 UUR**

Wouter Planteijdt, Beatrice van der Poel, Marijn Wijnands, Felix Maginn, J.B. Meyers, Ad Vanderveen, Dionys Breukers, Richard Heijerman en Gert Jan Blom.

Muzikanten die normaal niet met elkaar spelen. De opdracht van de VPRO: in vier dagen, in complete afzondering, nieuwe muziek componeren en daarmee een concert in Paradiso samenstellen. Het concert wordt live op radio 3FM en op internet uitgezonden. De televisie uitzending is zondag 19 juli om 23.00 uur op Ned.3. **Presentatie en huis-deejay's: de Easy Aloha's. Naprogramma in de bovenzaal met DJ Arnold Scheepmaker en live: Kirsten.** Entree f 15,-(excl. lidm. Paradiso), kaartverkoop bij de bekende voorverkoopadressen. **Kijk voor meer informatie op onze website: www.vpro.nl/moondive**

ontwerp: uleman@dietwee.nl

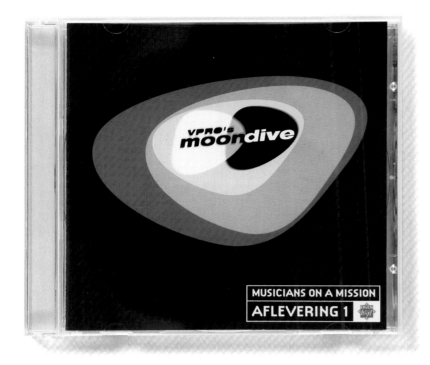

Musicians on a Mission

The VPRO public broadcasting company organized a series of meetings for musicians in a country house in the southernmost tip of the Netherlands. During one week, musicians from different backgrounds came together to compose new material which by the end of the week would be performed on stage at Paradiso in Amsterdam. VPRO's Moondive consisted of the reportage on the work sessions and the registration of the concert on television. The performance was also captured on CD for future listeners.

Wink was in charge of the presentation of the nights in Paradiso, and party art-director Arne Koefoed asked Dietwee to design a logo and a series of flyers and posters for Moondive – just as they had done for Hard Bop, BoomBoom and Get Stuffed. The logo was based on the eclipse of the moon, but it also referred to a guitar plectrum. To the title of the television program, they added a subtitle: 'Musicians on a Mission'. Abstraction was necessitated by the fact that nothing had yet been recorded when the logo was being designed. In each episode, the abstract background for the logo expressed the mix of styles that the programmers had in mind. It was the first time that Dietwee designed television titles, and Wink also included the logo in their stage design in Paradiso, which added to the overall consistancy. Moondive became quite popular and was granted a second season during the next summer.

25 JAAR FILMTHEATER 'T HOOGT PRESENTEERT

filmmarathon

9 FILMS VOOR SLECHTS 50 GULDEN
LOSSE KAARTEN PER FILM 10 GULDEN
DE KEUKEN BLIJFT OPEN VOOR O.A. DINER. ONTBIJT EN LUNCH

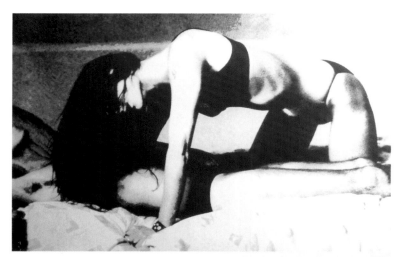

Cheap Chic

Filmtheater 't Hoogt was accustomed to producing its own posters on a photocopy machine. For their 25th year jubilee, they accordingly asked Dietwee to design a format that the employees could fill in themselves when announcing the films during the rest of that jubilee year. The solution lay in a less homemade approach, which also offered the possibility of giving 't Hoogt a more professional image. The condition that the posters be made with a low budget remained, however. Dietwee therefore decided to print the entire edition in silver, with the number 25, in advance. Each time a new poster was made, it was silk-screened over the silver print in accordance with a predetermined layout, but in a different colour. With limited means, the greatest possible variety had to be achieved, especially since more than one new poster often appeared in the city at the same time. The combination of a silver base with a photo silk-screened over it in a fluorescent colour produced surprising results, like with Natasha Kinski. When you looked at it from one angle the image appeared normal, and from another angle it seemed to be a transparency. The series was nominated that year for the Rotterdam Design Prize.

25 JAAR FILMTHEATER 'T HOOGT PRESENTEERT

GRATIS LUNCH–FILMPROGRAMMA

IN OKTOBER IEDERE DINSDAG EN VRIJDAG (m.u.v vr. 16)

Breng uw lunchpauze op ludieke wijze door en geniet (gratis!)
van een doorlopend filmprogramma met afleveringen van

Peyton Place,
Flintstones, The Monkeys,
The Beatles Cartoons

tussen 12.00 en 14.00 uur
De lunchzakjes mogen deze keer ook de zaal in

'**t Hoogt** | RESERVEREN 030 2328388, HOOGT 4, 3512 GW UTRECHT,
WEBSITE HTTP://WWW.XS4ALL.NL/~HOOGT

25 JAAR FILMTHEATER 'T HOOGT PRESENTEERT

SUNDAY JAZZ (gesponsord door Golden Coffee Box en Feedback)

ZONDAG 18 OKTOBER OM 16.00 UUR

Jazztrio Heleen S

HELEEN SCHUTTEVAÊR (pianiste/zangeres),
BART TARENSKEEN (bas), JOOST PATOCKA (drums)

'**t Hoogt** | RESERVEREN 030 2328388, HOOGT 4, 3512 GW UTRECHT,
WEBSITE HTTP://WWW.XS4ALL.NL/~HOOGT

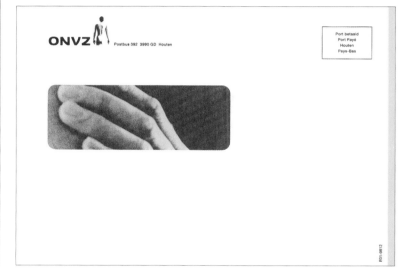

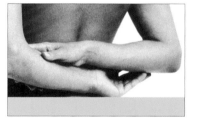

Corporate Man

After the first annual review with Dietwee, ONVZ decided to ask the agency to provide them with a new corporate image. In the briefing, the client expressed a strong preference for using the human body in the logo, because that would fit excellently with the company's thematic pay-off, 'Insure Your Most Precious Possession at ONVZ'. A purely typographical logo was simply not one of the options, although Dietwee had explicitly stated that preference. Seeing as the logo would automatically be combined with a photograph of the human body in all sorts of communications, the designers thought a typographical logo would be much clearer. In the end, however, the agency had to go along with the wishes of ONVZ, and so a human figure appeared in the logo after all: purposely a little vague as to whether it is a man or a woman, which is possible because the figure is seen from behind. Only where the logo coincides with a photograph in the various applications is this ambiguous figure absent, leaving simply the lettered logo after all.

Preciousness and Polaroids

The false start took three to four months, the final sprint barely two weeks. The second annual review that Dietwee made in collaboration with SYB Graphic Design for health insurer ONVZ was meant to be a 'feel good' book that answered the question of what people should do in order to remain healthy. Shortly before the final presentation to the client, the results proved to be too 'cute' and they radically altered the concept. Armed with a Polaroid camera and a notebook, the designers took to the streets to ask random passers-by what their most precious possession was, in accordance with ONVZ's slogan. The answers were very different: For some people it was their Breitling watch or their Riva boat, for others it was their mountain bike or their pet. And while for a lot of people it was their partner, in actuality, for most people their most valuable possession was indeed their health. In 160 photos and commentaries (some of which were made by photographer Bianca Pilet), 'Je kostbaarste bezit' (Your Most Precious Possession) gives an account of these last-minute street interviews.

Arie "Banaan" (72 jaar, eigenaar van een fruit- en snoepstal)

Mijn stalletje

Sharitza Henry (30 jaar, toerist)

Anton Hinse (50 jaar, stedebouwkundige)

Sygurd Cochius

Peter Paul Vos (32 jaar, fotograaf)

Katia Lucas (34 jaar, decor- en interieurontwerpster)

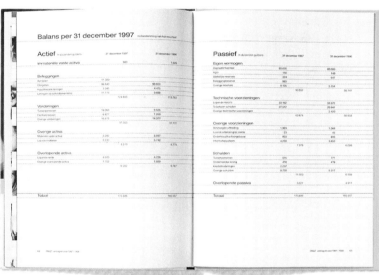

Balans per 31 december 1997

Actief in duizenden guldens	31 december 1997	31 december 1996	Passief in duizenden guldens	31 december 1997	31 december 1996
immateriële vaste activa	983	1.676	Eigen vermogen		

Piet Schreuder (26 jaar, werkt op een schapenboerderij)

Camiel van der Houven

Kiki de Jong-Luneau (27 jaar, foto-agente)

Maran van Scheppingen

Youri Thielen (13 jaar, scholier)

Suzanne Weijerman (16 jaar, scholiere)

Jo van der Mark (82 jaar, huisvrouw)

John Sandell (24 jaar, musicus)

Albert Wiglema (26 jaar, ondernemer)

Dhr. Glaudé

Said Chrifi (25 jaar, groenteman)

Carlo Schippers

Mevr. Kassenaar (68 jaar, huisvrouw)

Bianca Pilet (29 jaar, fotograaf)

Annemarieke Piers

Neil Cowan (31 jaar, timmerman)

C. A. Richel (53 jaar, toneelschrijf)

Joep Kervezee (47 jaar, kliplaer)

David Snellenberg

J. Vos (49 jaar, timmerman)
Mijn gezondheid

Dhr. W.A. Kolb
(51 jaar, witgoed detailist)
Mijn gezondheid

Ebbo de Jong
(52 jaar, directeur zorgverzekeraar)
Mijn gezondheid

Mirjam Blott (34 jaar,
hoofd presentatie/communicat
Gezondheid om optimaal van het leven te ge

Paulus Mooij (49 jaar, Antiquair)
Mijn gezondheid, want zonder gezondheid kun je
verder niets doen

Edith Scheenaard
(32 jaar, manager)
Mijn gezondheid, want zonder kun je niets

Richard Verwey (32 jaar,
bankmedewerker) Mijn gezondheid,
want als je niet gezond bent, heb je niets

G. Donk
(33 jaar, ondernemer/schoonm
De gezondheid van mijn dochters,

Annemieke Leeuwang
(27 jaar, psychologe) Mijn gezondheid

G. Wicart (69 jaar, advocaat)
Mijn gezondheid

W.E. Groeneweg
(41 jaar, docent)
Mijn gezondheid, want dan blijft mijn premie laag

I. Kroon
(58 jaar, schilder)
Mijn geestelijke en lichamelijke gezondheid

Roos Legvit
(22 jaar, studente medicijnen)
Gezondheid

Ellen Brouwer (16 jaar, scholiere)
Gezondheid, omdat ik van dichtbij heb meegemaakt dat
een vriendin ernstig ziek was

Frank Kempeneers
(32 jaar, bioloog) Ik twijfel tussen mijn liefde,
vrienden, familie en gezondheid

Marc Adema (30 jaar,
mode- en interieurontwerper)
Mijn gezondheid

Mathijs Kervezee
(16 jaar, scholier) Mijn gezondheid, want
anders kun je niet meer functioneren

Mw. Glaudé (62 jaar, huisvrouw)
Mijn gezondheid. Anders ben je er niet voor anderen

Rutger E.J. Brenninkmeyer
(31 jaar, ondernemer) Mijn gezondheid

Abe Chrifi (41 jaar, bedrijfs
M'n gezondheid, want als je echt niet gezond
heeft het geen zin om verder te leven.

Moni Ran
(30 jaar, eigenaar cadeauwinkel)

I. Jansen
(53 jaar, koopman)
Gezondheid kun je niet verdienen.

Dennis van Harten
(31 jaar, decorontwerper)
Mijn gezondheid.

Lisette van Velzen
(30 jaar, Televisieproducer)
M'n gezondheid, want zonder ben je niets.

Ronald van Leur (27 jaar,
bedrijfsleider) Gezondheid om zo lang
mogelijk de tijd even te genieten

Felix Williams
(23 jaar, vertegenwoordiger)
Mijn gezondheid.

Filip Otten
(33 jaar, inkoper mannenmode)
Gezondheid, omdat iedereen te vroeg dood gaat.

Harmen Liemburg
(31 jaar, grafisch ontwerper)
Geestelijke en lichamelijke gezondheid.

H. Nettlerott
(60 jaar, hotelmanager) Gezondheid.
Aan anderen kun je je brood niet verdienen.

M.L. van Egmond
(74 jaar, gepensioneerd)
Gezondheid.

Peter Roerink
(37 jaar, grafisch ontwerper)
Mijn gezondheid.

Leonie Sins
(24 jaar, administratief medewerkster)
Mijn gezondheid, want zonder doet het er niet meer toe.

C. Beemster (63 jaar, huisvrouw)
Mijn kinderen en kleinkinderen en dat we allemaal
gezond zijn

Willem van Duivenbode
(41 jaar, banketbakker)
Gezondheid.

Dinny Sijbers (57 jaar,
part-time verkoopster) Mijn gezondheid,
want als je ouder wordt wordt dat steeds belangrijker.

"Coos" Thöne (39 jaar,
directrice van vier modezaken)
Mijn gezondheid, maar vooral een gezonde geest.

Ineke Poortinga
(36 jaar, administrateur)
Mijn gezondheid

L. Bokstijn
(76 jaar, gepensioneerd)
Mijn gezondheid, want ik wil honderd worden.

Sandra Donk
(24 jaar, huisvrouw)
De gezondheid van mijn dochter.

T. Sijn (68 jaar, gepensioneerd)
Mijn man, kinderen en kleinkinderen, maar het
belangrijkste is dat ze gezond zijn.

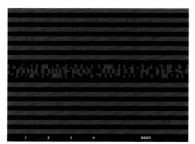

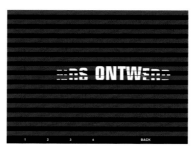

A Few of My Favourite Studios

BIS publishes a biannual review of the work of the members of the Association of Dutch Designers BNO, who are active as graphic, environmental or industrial designers. Approximately 350 agencies design their presentations themselves, while the book as a whole is designed by an agency especially chosen for that task. Dietwee assumed that directorial role in 1999. Quite likely, users will have but a few favourites amongst such a thick forest of pages. Which is why Dietwee wanted to paste a few arrows on the cover, to be used as page markers. But this was not technically feasible. The alternative was a gummed and perforated flyleaf, with which the reader could stick tabs, as it were, on each favourite page. Especially to protect these tabs, the cover of the book was extended by two centimetres. As to the rest, the Eurostile font was chosen for the editorial pages, and typographic illustrations imposed upon a strict grid were used to indicate each section. For the agency presentations, details about the agency and the work were purposely placed within a fairly dominant framework printed in metallic silver. This left as much design freedom as possible for the agencies in the space remaining. Additionally, this was the first occasion that the BNO book was accompanied by a CD-ROM featuring four interactive leaders, which had been developed in collaboration with Keez Duyves, now PIPS:Lab. At the time, Flash was still in its infancy, and for that reason, the leaders were programmed in Shockwave. This first interactive work by Dietwee exhibits clear stylistic similarities to their later Internet work for telecom provider Ben.

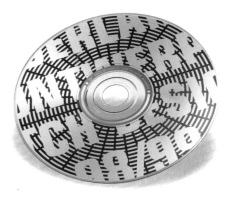

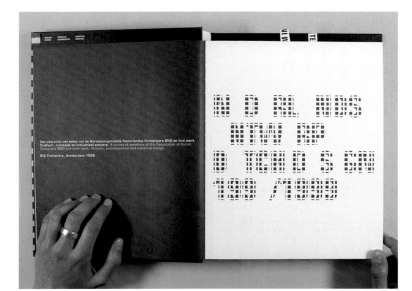

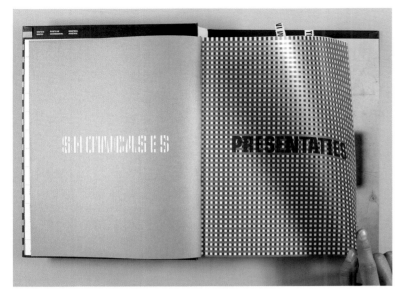

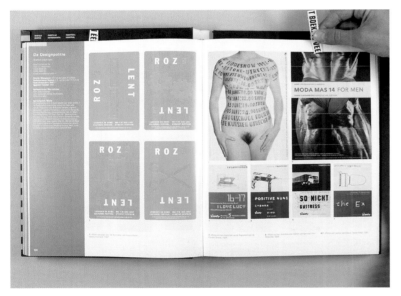

Personeelsjaarverslag 1998

Green[c]

Conditions did not lend themselves well for a prestigious annual personnel report. KPN had been privatised as a telecom concern in 1998, and the former monopolist had experienced intense competition from new telephone companies, whilst reorganizations had shaken up the company considerably. At the same time, the firm had gone to court and won exclusive rights to KPN-green (PMS 368), which other parties in the market were no longer allowed to use. Such were the two elements that finally determined the design: a cautious look at KPN's independent future and the KPN-green as copyright-protected colour. The ever-present green, as recorded by the photographer in photos of peppers, watering cans, leaves, apples, sunglasses, football fields, rubber boots and bottle recycling banks, was used in illustrations next to the texts. But do you dare place a picture of a bottle bank next to an article about outplacement, and does a barracks bag rhyme visually with the table of contents? At first glance, the photos appear to be scattered like gratuitous candy, but for the observant viewer the combinations are sometimes amusing, occasionally quite harsh, and at times even a little painful.

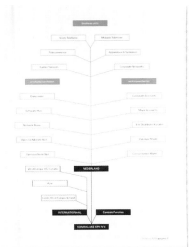

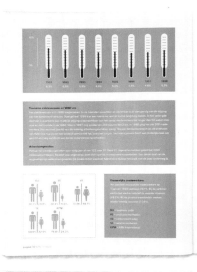
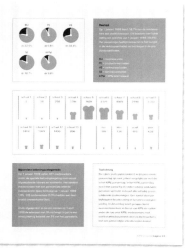

drum rhythm **night**

INDIAN ROPEMAN
SPACE RAIDERS
DJ SPARKY LIGHTBOURNE

Supporting dj's LX Pacific (Club de Ville) **Loes Lee** (Effenaar) **Svendex** (Winkel van Sinkel)

Thursday October 21 Club de Ville (Westergasfabriek), Amsterdam, 23.00 hrs. 020-681 30 68
Friday October 22 Effenaar, Eindhoven, 22.00 hrs. 040-243 55 59
Saturday October 23 Winkel van Sinkel, Utrecht, 24.00 hrs. 030-230 30 30
Admission f 15,-

design: martine eelman (www.dietwee.nl)

DRUM RHYTHM

More concert information
www.drumrhythm.com

Affinity

A new year of the monthly Drum Rhythm Nights
brought a more austere logo, but the graphic treat-
ment of the events did not change. The music of
the bands still dictated the visuals, and the colour
scheme remained limited to the Drum colours of red
and blue. But for the rest, almost anything was possible image-wise. The posters were made by various
designers in the studio, depending upon their affinity
with the performing artists and music styles.
The first Drum Rhythm CD, compiled by DJ LX Pacific,
was starkly designed with strong references to Drum
Rhythm again, due to its colour usage, but never any
real mentioning of its sponsor, tobacco company Drum.
Hence it was perceived as an independant label and
was sold as such.

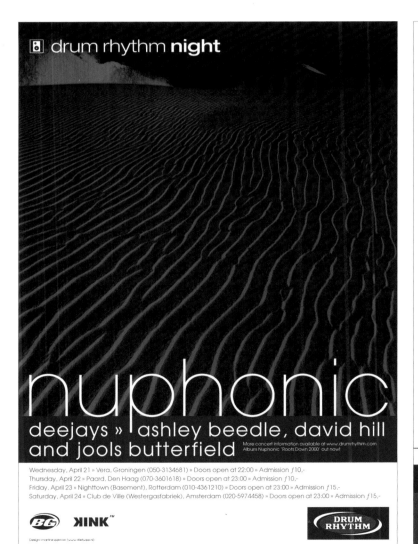

JONGERENFESTIVAL DE OPKOMST UTRECHT

THEATER / DANS / FILMS / CONCERTEN / TENTOONSTELLINGEN / CLINICS

DO 21 T/M ZO 24 OKTOBER 1999

OP VERSCHILLENDE LOCATIES IN DE STAD EMAIL: OPKOMST@LOKV.NL / INTERNET: WWW.OPKOMST.NL

BEL VOOR PROGRAMMA: (030) 2332328

Up & Coming

In order to give the ever-more professional youth festival 'De Opkomst' (Up & Coming) a look of its own, a new house style had to be created. This time, Dietwee decided to steer clear of figurative elements. The typography left only just enough room for a rising arrow, as a literal representation of the title of the festival. By working exclusively with two transparent PMS colours (yellow and blue) and therefore with the secondary colour of green as well, a rich, layered image could be achieved, which later also proved to be useful in other presentations for De Opkomst.

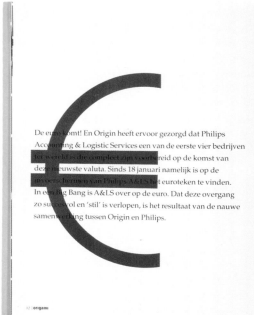

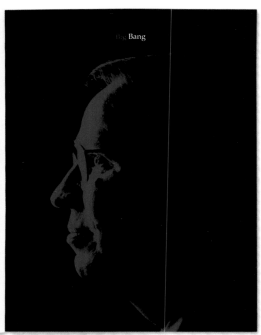

Magazine Itch

Magazine assignments are not just acquired on the basis of a good plan and good design, but mainly on the basis of relevant experience. That's the reasoning of most clients, at least. Experience provides security. And designers who lack that hardly get a chance to prove themselves as magazine-makers. Dietwee had lost an important pitch for that reason: the proposal was good, but the experience lacking. At that moment, BSO/Origin stepped in with its assignment for a new personnel magazine entitled Origami (believe it

or not, a contraction of Origin and Ami), addressed to the 5000 Dutch employees of the company. Although Dietwee had some doubts about the project, they could finally make a tri-weekly magazine, and it turned out to be quite an interesting job after all. When founder Eckart Wintzen left, the company had embarked upon an entirely new course and stopped working with Dietwee. Two years and many changes of management later, however, the new heads of the company decided that there were several aspects of

the former BSO identity which really did belong with the company after all, and so Dietwee was called back. The title was the one thing that was fixed; otherwise the agency had a great deal of freedom. In collaboration with Origin's editor-in-chief Ted van Hintum they came up with an editorial approach aimed at elevating Origami above the prevailing dullness in the corporate magazine world while at the same time avoiding the pitfalls of a club periodical. Conviviality and inanity were to make way for the

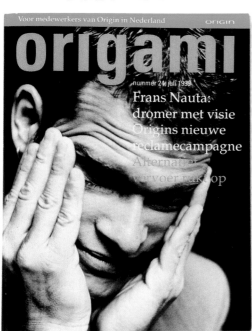

style employed by the ICT company: simple, open and clear. The company's house style dictated that the magazine had to be set in two fonts: Palatino and Univers. With this, too, the designers were better able to work than they had originally thought. As often as possible, the opening spreads of articles were designed separately, and from the very start photography played an important role in the concept. There was close collaboration with a large group of young photographers, quite a few of whom have made

a name for themselves since then. Their photos were to reflect the true-to-life quality that would characterize the magazine. Although Origami was printed in full colour, Dietwee usually employed black and white or duo-tone photography.
One feature copied from an earlier personnel magazine was a column called the Het Stokje (The Perch), in which workers nominated by their predecessors in the previous issue could introduce themselves. Here too, the change was chiefly in the photography.

Whereas in the previous publication the pictures had usually been awkward passport photos, due to the fact that employees lived and worked all over the country and it was financially unfeasible to send a photographer to them, an arrangement was made with photography shops throughout the country for Origami, so that people could stand in front of a white background and take a picture of themselves by pushing a button. This produced a distinctive yet homogeneous series of sympathetic portraits.

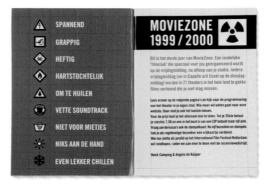

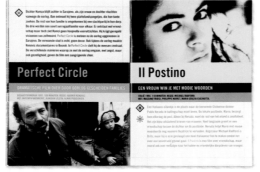

Don't!

The Moviezone program is an initiative of 20 film theatres to mobilize high school students to go to film classics suited for young people on quiet Friday afternoons, varying from Citizen Kane to The Big Lebowski – at a reduced price. For two years, an advertising agency had sought in vain for the proper tone of voice, but the communication hadn't worked to satisfaction. Dietwee had a different approach; they believed that the students were not being addressed in their own language. Instead of trying to encourage them, Dietwee decided to warn them off in order to increase the level of attraction. Thus the title became 'Beware of the Moviezone' and symbols of danger were introduced (the image of a film reel was transformed into the symbol for nuclear radiation) and every film was assigned a warning pictogram as classification. The program was printed in a booklet in free-card format, flyers were sent out and posters plastered freely across town. Crucial in the success of the initiative was the fact that teachers were encouraged to support the program in class by providing them with in-depth film information and study points were awarded for each visit to the film theatre.

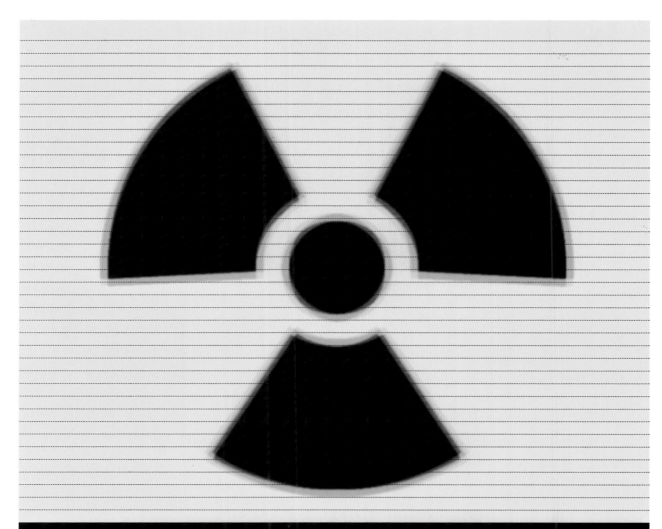

BEWARE OF THE
MOVIEZONE

GET SET FOR A FRIDAY AFTERNOON MELTDOWN AT YOUR LOCAL CINEMA AND PAY ONLY 7,50 (CJP/CKV 5,-) FOR A MINDBLOWING MOVIE EXPERIENCE THAT STICKS TO YOUR BRAIN FOR THE REST OF THE WEEK. ENTER THE MOVIEZONE AND CHARGE UP YOUR WEEKEND. THE ZONE RADIATES FROM 20 FILMTHEATERS THROUGHOUT THE COUNTRY. CHECK OUT YOURS FOR THE RIGHT TIME, OR VISIT THE MOVIESITE ⚡➞ WWW.MOVIEZONE.NL

MOVIEZONE ➞ ELKE VRIJDAGMIDDAG IN 20 FILMTHEATERS DOOR HET HELE LAND FILMS DIE JE NIET MAG MISSEN VOOR MAAR 7,50 (CJP/CKV 5,-)

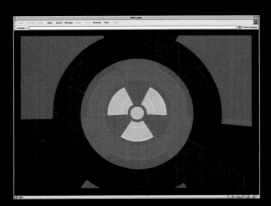

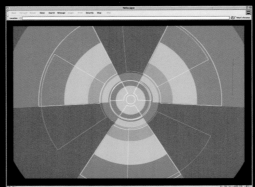

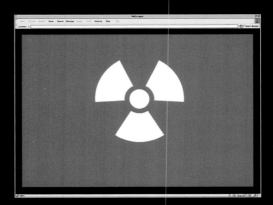

Classic Movies in HTML

The repositioning of Beware of the Moviezone went further than the traditional boundaries of graphic design. In order to be effective, the entire package of resources had to be attuned to the same goal. The design was employed as a strategic instrument in an entire concept of communication. For Dietwee, this meant that the need to offer extended services such as strategy and copywriting had only increased.

Therefore, in close collaboration with the client, the agency assembled extensive file folders of information for the teachers and created a website, which in addition to providing information about Moviezone, offered visitors the possibility to chat and let others know their reactions to the films they had seen. Because at that time too few computer users at schools had Flash at their disposal, the site was

made in HTML. Whereas in Flash any font can be used, HTML only offers Times or Arial (Helvetica). Since these were unacceptable, the website had to consist of an enormous amount of very labour-intensive typographical Gif illustrations, in order to remain true to the Moviezone design. This was so much work that Dietwee concluded that Flash should always be used for such projects in the future!

BEWARE OF THE MOVIEZONE

DE BESTE FILMS VOOR MAAR 7,50

DE BOEKVERFILMING ➔ FUNNY GAMES ➔ TWENTYFOURSEVEN

MADE IN HONG KONG ➔ FESTEN ➔ WHO THE HELL IS JULIETTE?

IL POSTINO ➔ CHUNKING EXPRESS ➔ LA VIE RÊVÉE DES ANGES

LOLA RENNT ➔ PERFECT CIRCLE ➔ WILD AT HEART ➔ GUMMO

KURT & COURTNEY ➔ LAMERICA ➔ HANA-BI ➔ CITIZEN KANE

CITY OF THE LOST CHILDREN ➔ THE BIG LEBOWSKI ➔ GADJO DILO

CHECK YOUR LOCAL CINEMA

ALKMAAR **FILMTHEATER PROVADJA** / AMSTERDAM **RIALTO** / APELDOORN **FILMTHEATER GIGANT** / ARNHEM **FILMHUIS ARNHEM**
BREDA **CHASSÉ CINEMA** / CAPELLE A/D IJSSEL **ISALA THEATER** / DELFT **FILMHUIS LUMEN** / DEN BOSCH **FILMTHEATER JEROEN**
DEN HAAG **HAAGS FILMHUIS** / DEVENTER **FILMHUIS DE KEIZER** / EINDHOVEN **PLAZA FUTURA** / ENSCHEDE **FILMTHEATER CONCORDIA**
GRONINGEN **FILMCENTRUM POELESTRAAT** / HILVERSUM **FILMTHEATER HILVERSUM** / LEEUWARDEN **FILMHUIS LEEUWARDEN**
NIJMEGEN **CINEMARÏENBURG** / ROTTERDAM **LANTAREN/VENSTER** / TILBURG **FILMHUIS LOUIS** / UTRECHT **'T HOOGT** / VLISSINGEN **CINECITY**

| SPANNEND | GRAPPIG | HEFTIG | HARTS-TOCHTELIJK | OM TE HUILEN | VETTE SOUNDTRACK | NIET VOOR MIETJES | NIKS AAN DE HAND | EVEN LEKKER CHILLEN |

HAAL HET MOVIEZONE MAGAZINE 1999/2000 BIJ DE THEATERS
OF BEZOEK DE MOVIESITE. BELLEN KAN OOK > 030 2312216

 www.moviezone.nl

MOVIEZONE IS EEN PRODUCTIE VAN FILMTHEATER 'T HOOGT. MOGELIJK GEMAAKT DOOR >
NEDERLANDS FONDS VOOR DE FILM > MINISTERIE VAN OC&W, AFDELING CULTUUR EN SCHOOL > VSB FONDS > PRINS BERNHARD FONDS >
NFC STICHTING MARKETING EN COMMUNICATIE > THUISKOPIE FONDS > CJP > DE VOLKSKRANT. **GRAPHIC DESIGN** > ROBIN ULEMAN (WWW.DIETWEE.NL)

Communication Directors

The collaboration between Sybren Kuiper of SYB Graphic Design and Dietwee had taken shape in the previous two ONVZ annual reports. And it was during this third annual report that it became clear for Ron Faas and Tirso Francés that Dietwee should start operating in a different manner. What they had in mind, in fact, was the role of art directors, somewhat comparable with how an advertising agency functions. Such an approach would necessarily also have consequences for the latest ONVZ annual report that the two agencies were preparing. In addition to reporting on the state of affairs at

health insurer ONVZ, the new report 'hoe gaat het...' (How is it going...) was supposed to present a questionnaire about health. A thing devoid of humour until that point. But as the designers determined the concept, they conceived of the type of humour that drove EGBG's designer Martijn Engelbregt in his fascination for questionnaires. And so calling in Engelbregt himself was a foregone conclusion. Faas and Francés did the 'casting' and then withdrew to the background to operate as art directors. Sybren Kuiper and Martijn Engelbregt acted as designers for the report. Together they developed a

scheme of serious yet entertaining questions about health that would steer readers through the annual report in an individualized manner. Depending on their answers, readers finally arrived at a point in the list of results that typified their personal health situation. Lastly, these results could be entered and compared with others on the website, www.hoegaathet.nl, which remained online for one year.

Ron and Tirso discovered that, like advertising agencies, Dietwee had no problems in calling in outside designers when a concept asks for it and that this could lead to excellent results.

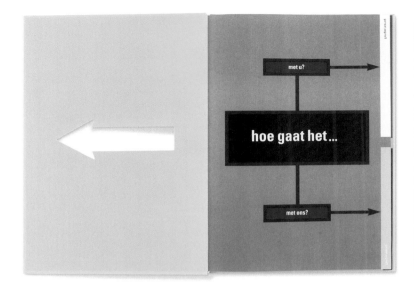

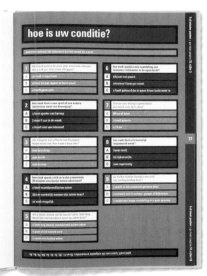

Zorgpas

Het ZorgPas Initiatief (ZPI), waarin ONVZ participeert, heeft begin 1998 een businessplan opgesteld voor de aanleg van een landelijke en neutrale elektronische snelweg voor de zorgsector, gekoppeld aan een zorgpas voor alle verzekerden. Vereenvoudiging van het declaratieverkeer en de administratieve processen in de zorgsector was onder andere de insteek. Het businessplan bleek onvoldoende draagvlak te hebben. Door een herbezinning op de plannen lijkt nu bij de verschillende partijen een breed draagvlak te kunnen worden bereikt. Via fasering met separate besluitvormingsmomenten kunnen de projectrisico's beter onder controle worden gehouden. Ook is de functionaliteit op onderdelen aangepast.

De winst voor zorgverzekeraars valt te behalen via een efficiënter declaratieverkeer. De particuliere ziektekostenverzekeraars reageerden enigszins teleurgesteld op het besluit om deze functie pas in een latere fase van het project te realiseren.

Naar verwachting zal in mei 1999 een plan van aanpak door de Stuurgroep Zorgpas worden opgeleverd. Naast zorgverzekeraars participeren hierin ook aanbieders en patiënten/consumenten. Na goedkeuring start eind 1999 een proef in de regio Eemland. ONVZ zal de ontwikkelingen ten aanzien van de zorgpas nauwlettend volgen. Vooralsnog ziet het ernaar uit dat dit in 1999 geen consequenties voor ONVZ zal hebben.

42

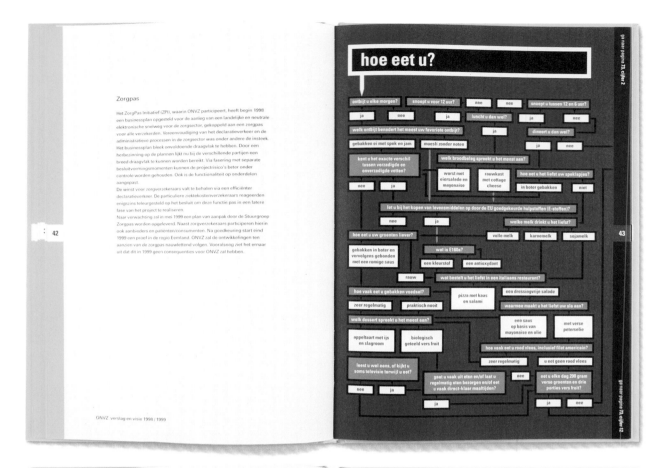

43

Herstructurering Ziekenfondswet

Het vorige kabinet heeft een pakket van maatregelen doorgevoerd, dat tot herstructurering van de ziekenfondsverzekering moet leiden. Deze maatregelen waren voornamelijk gericht op het verbeteren van de verzekeringspositie van personen van 65 jaar en ouder.

Als eerste stap is een wet in werking getreden waarmee de inkomensgrens voor de ziekenfondsverzekering voor AOW-gerechtigden fors werd verhoogd. Daardoor konden meer ouderen ziekenfondsverzekerd worden. Als gevolg van deze wijzigingen komt de instroom in de ziekenfondsverzekering van het aantal personen van 65 jaar en ouder op circa 90.000. Dit aantal was aanvankelijk geraamd op 200.000. Dit blijkt uit cijfers van de Ziekenfondsraad.

Op 1 augustus 1997 trad een wijziging van de Ziekenfondswet in werking waardoor nieuwe studenten van wie de ouders ziekenfondsverzekerd zijn, niet meer gratis meeverzekerd zijn. Zij dienden een particuliere ziektekostenverzekering af te sluiten. De schatting was dat uiteindelijk, na verloop van vier jaar, ongeveer 185.000 mensen minder van de gratis meeverzekering gebruik zullen maken.

Voor 1997 werd het aantal uitstromende studenten geraamd op 75.000. Volgens de Ziekenfondsraad dient deze schatting neerwaarts te worden bijgesteld. De uitstroom moet wellicht op ten minste de helft van 75.000 gesteld worden. Waarschijnlijk is een groot aantal jongeren op eigen titel ziekenfondsverzekerd in plaats van meeverzekerd.

24

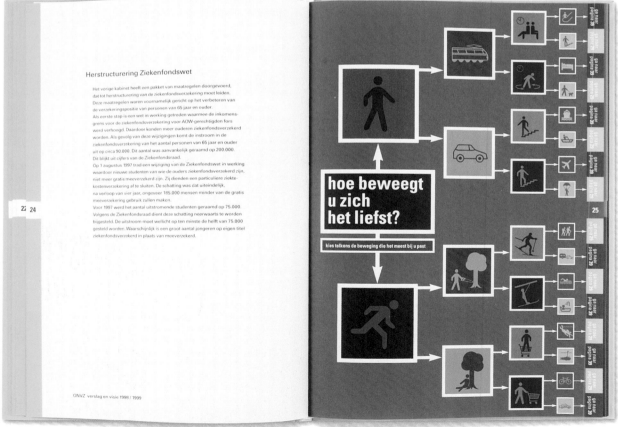

25

**waar zit
u met uw
hoofd?**

Pressure Cooker Creativity

Ad agency KesselsKramer phoned on December 3rd, 1999. Via an indirect route they had finally been commissioned to launch a new Dutch mobile telecom provider. Exactly two months were left for developing a house style, website, brochures and advertising. So far, there was no more than a strong concept, a name (Ben), a logo (in Trade Gothic) and a colour (blue); but as art director Erik Kessels had correctly assumed, those elements fit right in with Dietwee's style and mentality, so he asked them to concentrate on the corporate identity, website and brochures. Kesselskramer's concept of a telephone company with a personal identity who keeps things simple is an interesting one. 'Ben' in Dutch has a double meaning. It is both the name of a person, Ben, and the Dutch word for 'am' as in 'I am'. So 'Ik ben Ben' translates as 'I am Ben'.

'Ik Ben er voor jouw' translates as 'I am there for you'. In the meantime, Ben was working night and day on the product package and pricing, so product development, design, marketing and communication were done at one and the same time. And all in eight weeks! The corporate identity was in fact the simple part of the assignment. In the spirit of Ben, Dietwee added small touches to the corporate identity, such as the fact that the words 'Hello, I am' were printed in reverse on the back of company letters, so that on the front it read 'Hello, I am Ben' in combination with the logo when held toward the light. On one side of Ben business cards, a person was always introduced with his first name only ('I am Luuk'), using the double meaning of the word Ben, thus emphasizing the personal and unconventional character of the company.

Simplicity in a Complex World

Ben was on a mission to keep things simple in the new, complex world of mobile telecommunications. An uncomplicated but efficient pricing system which was very different from their competitors was therefore important for their website. If consumers are almost persuaded to go with a brand-new company, price can be the deciding factor. The clearer that simple message came across, the greater the chance of success. Dietwee's first large website started with a virtually blank 'letter of credit'. The web pages had to uphold the identity of the brand - while that identity was still developing - through great clarity, abundant use of photos and bold typography. But what do you do with a corporate identity that is mainly couched in Trade Gothic when (again) that font is not supported by HTML?

Flash was still not quite universal enough, so just as they had done with 'Moviezone', the designers constructed the site by using many typographical Gif illustrations for all the headings. That way, the very distinct typographical house style was optimally retained. Within the agreed-upon eight weeks, Ben was online and Dietwee had built their first really large site, which received more than 10,000 visitors per day in the first month.

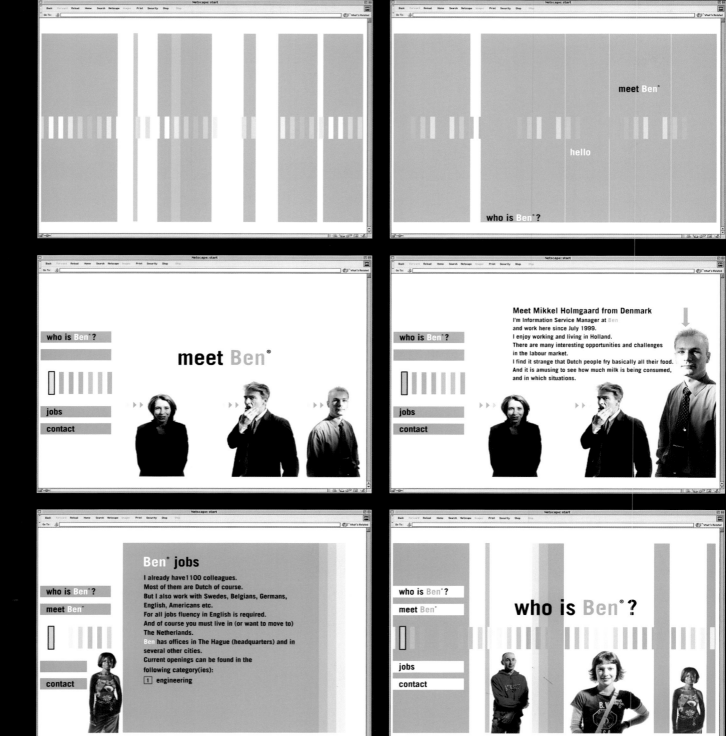

Flash Ben

It soon became obvious that the dynamics of the market required a site that could be frequently revised and refined. That was very labour-intensive, since in order to optimalize the 'Ben-feeling' all the headings were in the Trade Gothic font and placed on the website as Gif illustrations.

The introduction of Flash meant that a labour-intensive construction process could be cut short: The designers of the Ben site now had a new set of graphic tools to work with. Ben.nl was the first large site in the Netherlands to be totally realized in Flash. Because of this, for example, navigating could be

done at floating vertical sliding bars, and the problem with fonts like Trade Gothic was solved in one fell swoop. This technical freedom of designing gave the site an architecture that made quick alterations possible and additionally offered individual leeway to the four different designers who daily administered the site.

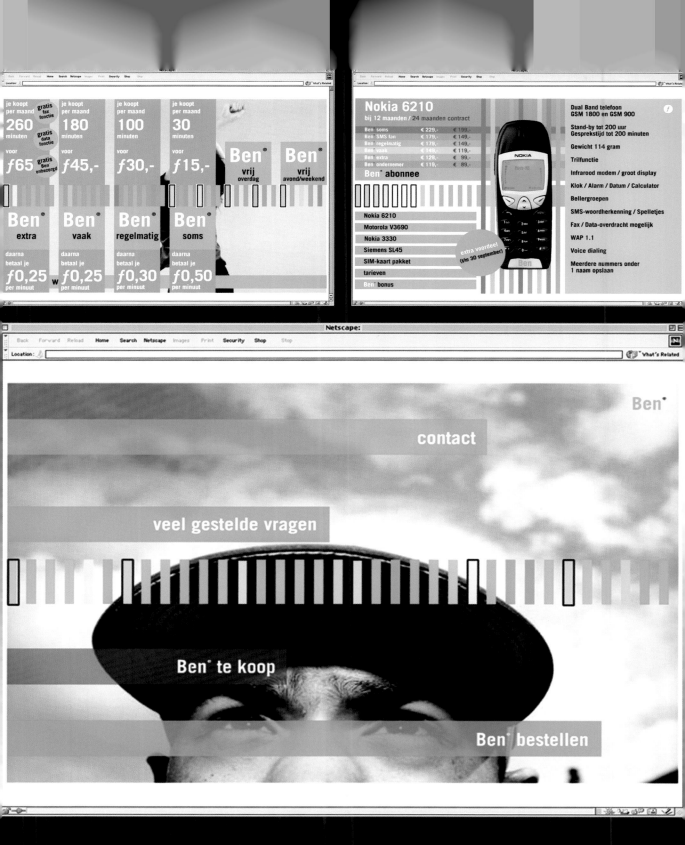

Because Ben's identity had been further developed in the meantime, the visual language could link up better with Ben's image. Simplicity, openness and directness were the key concepts in the image that Ben projected. On top of that, Kesselskramer introduced playfulness in advertisements for the brand, and

it is precisely this light element which has proven useful to the website. New campaigns and promotions can totally change the look of the site each week, because switching photos in the background is a simple matter, whilst the outer framework scarcely needs adjustment. Within the very extensive amount

of information on offer, special the Ben Olympic and Ben Dealer main both in terms of content and desig For quite a long time the site was visited websites of the Netherlands much bigger KPN telecom websi

Ben° olympisch

Als partner in sport ondersteunt Ben° de Olympische ploeg op weg naar Sydney. En Ben° steunt ook individuele sporters zoals de trampolinespringer Alan Villafuerte. Klik op de cirkels voor meer informatie.

Ben° olympisch

Ben° Olympische Talentendag

wie is Ben°

Hier vind je informatie over bellen en gebeld worden met Ben°. Voor dit overzicht van alle Ben° producten en diensten klik je op de streepjes.

in english

hallo, ik ben Maarten van der Linden

Ik heb een eigen bedrijf in meubel- en scheepsbouw. Een druk bestaan, want ik train zo'n 28 uur per week voor de lichte heren dubbel twee. Roeien dus. En dan hou ik ook nog van reizen en zeilen. Nu ben ik druk met de voorbereiding op het WK in Luzern en Canada en de Olympische Spelen in Sydney. Als ik 's avonds, samen met mijn vriendin Marleen, tapas met een koud biertje voor me heb, kan mijn avond niet meer stuk. JJ Cale mag voor de muziek zorgen.

Ben° olympisch

terug   sporters

Roeien: lichte dubbel twee

Belangrijke prestatie:

Olympische Spelen Atlanta 1996: zilver

Ben°WAP

GSM diensten
SMS diensten
Ben°-online
Ben° nummerbehoud
Ben°WAP
beltegoed opwaarderen

begin met Ben°WAP

Tarieven

Diensten

Netwerk

Ben° zakelijk

Ben° biedt veel extra diensten, services en een garantie. Alles om het de zakelijke beller gemakkelijker te maken. Klik op een van de items voor meer informatie.

Bestellen

Contact

Ben°-beheer

GSM-diensten
SMS-diensten
Ben°-beheer
Ben° onbezorgd
Ben° nummerbehoud
Ben° fax- en dataservice
Ben° bulk SMS

Panel 1 (top-left)

Netscape: Ben-Dealer

Ben® dealer

Panel 2 (top-right)

Netscape: Ben-Dealer

nieuws

ik Ben® dealer

Bij u kopen klanten hun Ben® product. En bij u komen ze met vragen of problemen. Daarom wil Ben® u als dealer goed informeren. Deze website helpt u daarbij. U vindt informatie over Ben® zelf, winkel- en verkoop-adviezen, producten, diensten, specifieke problemen en adresgegevens. Bovendien kunt u hier de laatste radiocommercials horen en de laatste televisiecommercials bekijken.

Ben® hecht waarde aan de mening van anderen. Dus als u suggesties heeft voor de inhoud van deze website, laat het Ben® dan weten. Ben® wenst u veel succes met uw verkoop en service.

oasys   login

Panel 3 (middle-left)

Netscape: Ben-Dealer

On line activeren; sneller mobiel

Waarom is on line activeren zo interessant? Ben® klanten on line activeren, gaat niet alleen veel sneller. Maar is ook nog efficiënter.

Met het on line activatie-systeem van Ben® ontglipt u niets bij het activeren. Uw klant is dus sneller mobiel.

Wilt u on line activeren? Heeft u vragen over de werking van dit systeem? Neem dan contact op met uw Ben® verkoop- of winkeladviseur. Of bel met Ben® Dealer Verkoopondersteuning: 0800-8106. Zij helpen u graag verder.

← Door naar OASYS

Panel 4 (middle-right)

Netscape: Ben-Dealer

Motorola V3690	↘
Motorola V100	↘
Nokia 6210	↘
Panasonic GD93	↘
Philips Ozeo	↘
Nokia 3330	↘
Siemens SL45	↘

Siemens SL45

Type	Dual Band telefoon GSM 1800 en GSM 900
Gewicht	88 gram
Batterij	150 uur standby 200 minuten spreektijd
Extra	Trilfunctie / Klok / Alarm / Datum WAP 1.1 / MP3-speler (standaard ca. 30 min.) Voicedail, voice activating Agenda (synchronisatie met o.a. Outlook) Verwisselbare geheugenkaart (standaard 32MB) Picture messaging (Siemens onderling!) Sms-woordherkenning / infrarood / memorecorder Card-Explorer (overzicht v.d. geheugenkaart) Fax / Data-overdracht mogelijk

prijzen →

nieuws   product info   promotie   Ben® helpt   events   Ben®

Panel 5 (bottom-left)

Netscape: Ben-Dealer

Ben® soms	Ben® regelmatig	Ben® vaak
€ 7,50	€ 15,-	€ 22,50
30 minuten per maand	75 minuten per maand	150 minuten per maand
daarna € 0,25 per minuut	daarna € 0,20 per minuut	daarna € 0,15 per minuut
SMS-tekstbericht € 0,19	SMS-tekstbericht € 0,19	SMS-tekstbericht € 0,19
Ben® extra	Ben® ondernemer	Ben® SMS fan
		€ 15,-
€ 35,-	€ 42,50	100 berichten per maand
300 minuten per maand	360 minuten per maand	daarna € 0,15 per SMS
daarna € 0,12 per minuut	daarna € 0,12 per minuut	bellen € 0,20 per minuut
SMS-tekstbericht € 0,19	SMS-tekstbericht € 0,19	starttarief € 0,05
		Ben®WAP € 0,15 per minuut

→ Toestellen
Tarieven buitenland
Tarieven naar satelliettelefoons
GSM-diensten
SMS-diensten
Servicenummers
Netwerk
Algemene Voorwaarden

nieuws   product info   promotie   Ben® helpt   events   Ben®

Panel 6 (bottom-right)

Netscape: Ben-Dealer

Ben® WAP

Ben® WAP biedt de klant toegang tot speciale WAP-pagina's op het internet via de WAP-telefoon. Via zijn WAP-telefoon kan de klant op elk gewenst moment alle openbare WAP-pagina's bekijken. Zo kan hij bijvoorbeeld nieuws- of file-informatie opvragen, cd's bestellen, spelletjes spelen en nog veel meer. Bovendien kan de Ben® klant gebruik maken van diverse speciale Ben® WAP-diensten, zoals het bekijken van rekening-informatie, het versturen van beltonen, het lezen en versturen van e-mail en het bijhouden van zijn agenda. Voor optimaal gebruik en service van Ben® WAP heeft de klant een door Ben® ondersteunde WAP-telefoon nodig. De lijst met WAP-telefoons die Ben® heeft getest is uitgebreid en er komen steeds meer telefoons bij.

volgende →

producten   toestellen   diensten   internet   online   beheer   wap   onbezorgd   prom

this friday
upclub
frankie d
www.nachtwinkel.nl

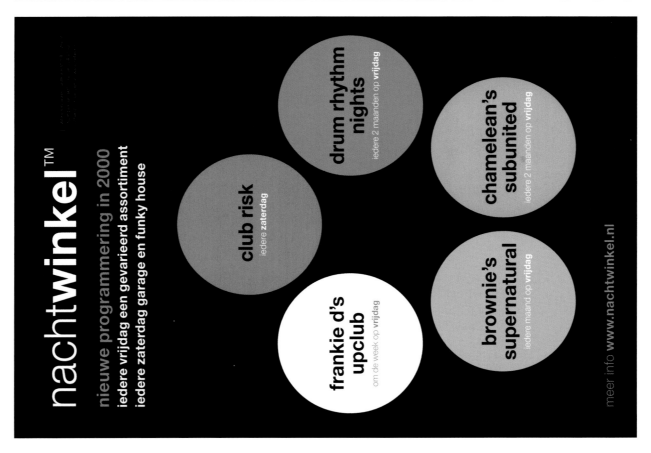

nachtwinkel™

om de vrijdag
**frankie d's
upclub**

elke zaterdag
club risk
garage + funky house

meer info www.nachtwinkel.nl
winkel van sinkel >> oudegracht 158 >> utrecht >> ingang aan de werf >> aanvang 00.00 uur
ontwerp robin uleman (www.dietwee.nl)

nachtwinkel™

nieuwe programmering in 2000
iedere vrijdag een gevarieerd assortiment
iedere zaterdag garage en funky house

**drum rhythm
nights**
iedere 2 maanden op **vrijdag**

club risk
iedere **zaterdag**

**chamelean's
subunited**
iedere 2 maanden op **vrijdag**

**frankie d's
upclub**
om de week op **vrijdag**

**brownie's
supernatural**
iedere maand op **vrijdag**

meer info www.nachtwinkel.nl

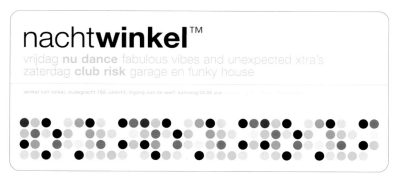

Carte Blanche

In the nightlife circuit, contemporary clubs have to constantly innovate and evolve to remain successful. By 2000, Winkel van Sinkel's creative director Didier Prince decided that the idea of giving the Nachtwinkel (Night Shop) the gestalt of a nightlife supermarket needed upgrading. Dietwee requested, and received, carte blanche in determining a renewed identity, which emphasized the brand more than previously. Designer Robin Uleman took inspiration from the designs made in the '70s by Otto Treuman for the Bijenkorf, a large Dutch department store. The language became simpler, the images kept as elementary as possible. The scope of the design, in fact, was partially determined by the functionality of the website. Only what could translate well into the digital medium was given a place on the posters, flyers and membership cards, thus producing an optimally integrated look.

nachtwinkel™

juli

03 10 17 24 01 0

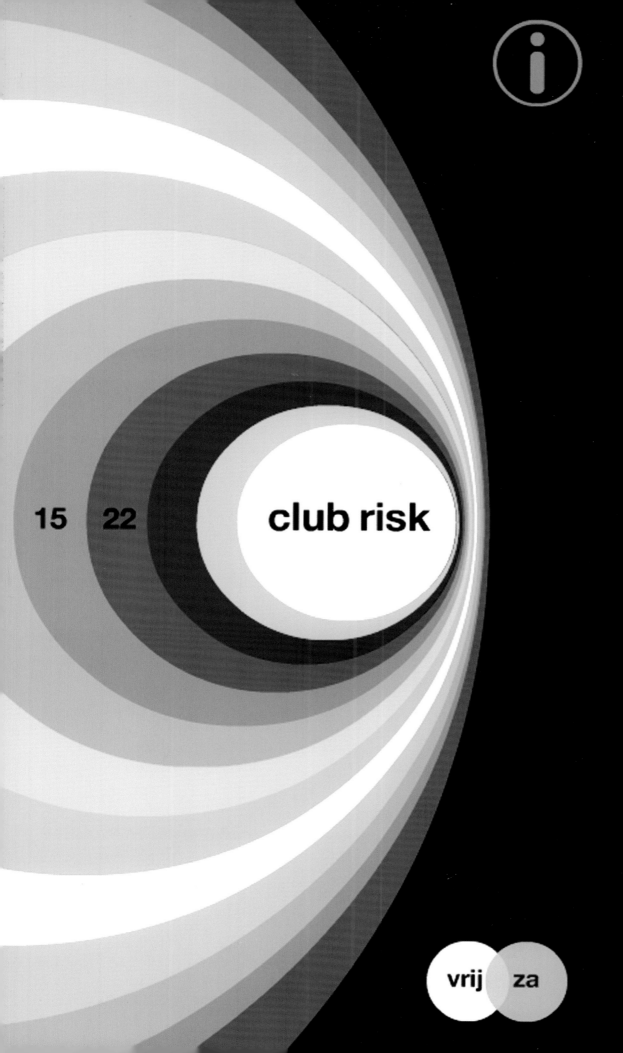

15 22

club risk

vrij za

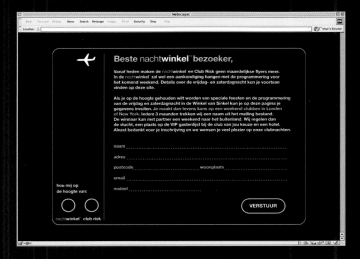

Form Over Content

The liveliness of a site and of its interaction with visitors is closely connected to the 'newsworthiness' of what it has to offer. In other words: content largely determines the form. Fridays and Saturdays in the Nachtwinkel had their own programming: the alternative dance scene on Fridays and the more commercial Techno House evenings on Saturdays. Using a dynamic navigation system, web visitors could subscribe to the Nachtwinkel mailing list, experience the music themselves and obtain information about the acts featured that month. Movement and sound were totally integrated in a fresh and astoundingly simple design: an optimally successful collaboration between the primary identity created by Robin Uleman and the dynamic navigation of Dirkjan Brummelman. The website was nominated for several design awards both in the Netherlands and Germany as well as in New York City.

Choices

KPN Telecom experienced a turbulent last year of the millennium. Many players (like Ben) had made the market for mobile telephony unsafe and therefore KPN personnel were suddenly offered many alternative workplaces. The company had difficult choices to make in order to safeguard its future. Within KPN, employees had to choose one of its four operating companies – the four 'scoops' as they were called within the firm.

The cover of the 1999 Annual Personnel Report was a tongue-in-cheek reference to that metaphor. The colours of the ice cream correspond to the house colours of the four most important telephone providers in the Netherlands.

The most significant internal change during 1999, however, was that employees were given the chance to determine their own career planning: shorter hours, more salary or more pension, full-time or part-time jobs etc. Within these options

were also choices. The annual report, commissioned by the works council, could therefore have but one theme. Employees were randomly interviewed by telephone as to the most important choice of the past year. Moving to the country for instance, or spending more time with family, were directly linked to the career choices they had made at KPN, such as working less hours. A photographer was sent out to illustrate those stories, which were flanked by the corporate reports.

Due to the company's financial hard times, Dietwee decided, just as last year, not to spend too much money on paper and binding. Therefore they had the review printed on recycled paper with a self-cover, so that it felt more like a magazine than a glossy (and exorbitantly expensive) annual report.

tandwiel

omvang	materialen	locatie
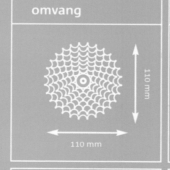	roestvrijstaal	

gewicht	herkomst	eigenschappen
625 gram	Nederland	degelijk, slijtvast, hard

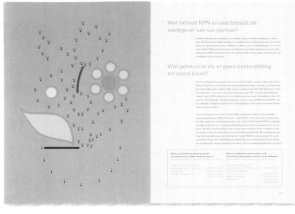

Visual Metaphors

After two successful internal annual reports, Dietwee was asked by KPN to take charge of other forms of personnel communications for the company. A series of internal brochures for the KPN Personnel Department presented such themes as Job Appreciation, Child Care and Competencies. For each subject, a visual metaphor was developed and elaborated in full-page illustrations. The KPN house style, designed by Studio Dumbar, dictated the use of several graphic symbols on the covers, and Univers as the body type, but nonetheless offered sufficient room to conceive and work out a coherent communicative visual concept. When the guidelines concerning the house style grew even stricter, however, and the requirements for using specially designed corporate fonts were adapted to limit freedom still further, the designers did not feel they had enough elbow-room anymore therefore Dietwee decided to end the collaboration.

Alles weten over spiergroepen?

Fysiotherapie
Ook Hogeschool van Utrecht

Meer weten over Fysiotherapie of een van de 70 andere opleidingen/afstudeerrichtingen aan de Faculteiten Gezondheidszorg, Natuur & Techniek, Economie & Management, Educatieve Opleidingen, Communicatie & Journalistiek en Sociaal Agogische Opleidingen?

Kom naar de Studiebeurs
op 28, 29 en 30 september.
Jaarbeurs Utrecht, stand 4C17.
Kijk op www.hvu.nl

Hogeschool
van Utrecht

Alles weten over vreemde talen?

Opleiding leraar/tolk Nederlandse Gebarentaal
Ook Hogeschool van Utrecht

Meer weten over opleiding leraar/tolk Nederlandse Gebarentaal of een van de 70 andere opleidingen/afstudeerrichtingen aan de Faculteiten Sociaal Agogische Opleidingen, Economie & Management, Educatieve Opleidingen, Gezondheidszorg, Communicatie & Journalistiek en Natuur & Techniek?

Kom naar de Studiebeurs
op 28, 29 en 30 september.
Jaarbeurs Utrecht, stand 4C17.
Kijk op www.hvu.nl

Hogeschool
van Utrecht

Alles weten over acné?

Huidtherapie
Ook Hogeschool van Utrecht

Meer weten over Informatica / Telematica of een van de 70 andere opleidingen/afstudeerrichtingen aan de Faculteiten Natuur & Techniek, Gezondheidszorg, Economie & Management, Educatieve Opleidingen, Communicatie & Journalistiek en Sociaal Agogische Opleidingen?

Kom naar de Studiebeurs
op 28, 29 en 30 september.
Jaarbeurs Utrecht, stand 4C17.
Kijk op www.hvu.nl

Hogeschool
van Utrecht

Alles weten over de onder- en bovenbouw?

Lerarenopleiding Basis Onderwijs
Ook Hogeschool van Utrecht

Meer weten over Lerarenopleiding Basis Onderwijs of een van de 70 andere opleidingen/afstudeerrichtingen aan de Faculteiten Educatieve Opleidingen, Sociaal Agogische Opleidingen, Economie & Management, Gezondheidszorg, Communicatie & Journalistiek en Natuur & Techniek?

Kom naar de Studiebeurs
op 28, 29 en 30 september.
Jaarbeurs Utrecht, stand 4C17.
Kijk op www.hvu.nl

Hogeschool
van Utrecht

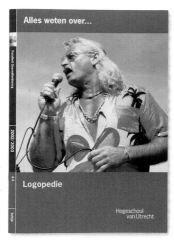

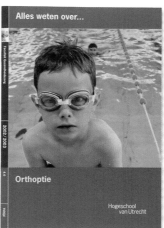

Balancing Act

In recent years, schools and training courses for higher vocational education have drawn together in increasingly greater clusters. And mutual competition for new students is tougher than ever. Every big city in the Netherlands has its higher vocational institution or academy, which by and large remains an island empire of sharply differing educational training programs in the fields of technique, art, healthcare, economics, communication, education, etc. In order to recruit students for all these schools, however, the academies prefer to present a single front. As does the Utrecht School of Higher Education (HvU), which asked Dietwee to serve as its advertising agency, wanting a recruitment campaign which was more tongue-in-cheek than they had been used to. Because of its decentralised structure the HvU furnished no less than 18 contact persons for consultation. Each faculty raised other problems and considerations in the discussions with Dietwee. One had over-capacity, another could barely handle the flood of students. The campaign was a 'balancing act' in the best sense of the word: between uniformity and recognizability; between earnestness and humour; between content and image; between design and advertisement.

The concept and realization of the campaign 'Alles weten over...' (Knowing everything about...) consisted of 18 different billboards, 64 brochures, 12 different free-cards, and a website coupled with an extensive Content Management System. The art editors made associative links between the content of the specific educational programs and the youths' daily environment. They explicitly tried not to imitate them, but to show that the HvU understands its target group. The images are 'contrary' enough to be noticeable and are presented in a respectable format that supports the identity of the school.

Dietwee developed a communications strategy which meets the need for information in an intelligent manner. The posters attract high school graduates by a subtle feeling for humour, thus making the initial contact. In order to further strengthen its ties with potential students, more information is available through the website in a clear design that enlarges upon the HvU campaign. Finally, the brochures give those who are serious a detailed insight into the structure of a particular training system, while still implicitly retaining the sense of a school with a realistic attitude toward the world close to that of its students.

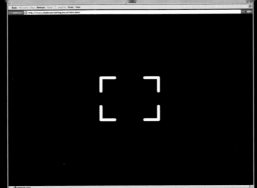

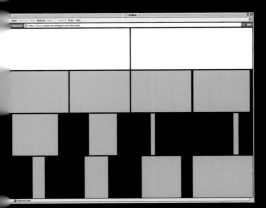
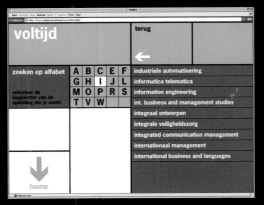
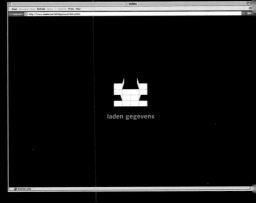

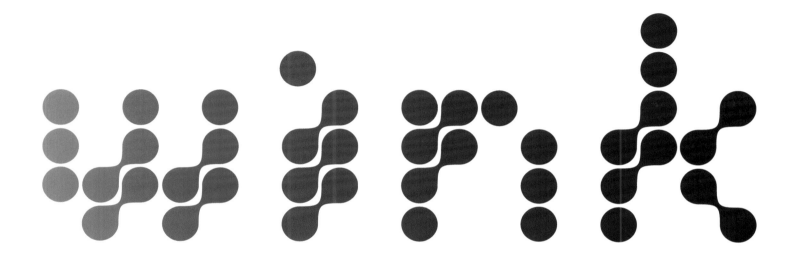

The Right Mood

Factor H does 'mood marketing'. The H refers to
the acronym 'Horeca' – the Hotel, Restaurant and
Catering business, in which many different moods
exist. Factor H advises brands and businesses about
the best way to establish a position for their product
within the various aspects of this branch, and be-
lieves that more interaction with the public is one of
the most effective means to do so.

In order to make it clear that the 'Horeca' branch has
various identities, and thus that the consumer also
has various possibilities to choose from, Dietwee

designed a house style in which the H was designed
in 112 different ways. All of these H's are provided
on sheets of stickers, so that when employees send
out letters, they can choose an appropriate H for
each. Contacts receive a business card and the
sheet of stickers so they can determine the appropriate mood for the company themselves, thus creating interaction on a first level.

Funky

Years ago, Wink had introduced the Hard Bop parties
in Utrecht, for which Dietwee made the first flyers,
and later on the two companies had again worked
closely together on BoomBoom, the Rebellenclub,
Get Stuffed, VPRO's Moondive, and Drum Rhythm.
As the years went by, the company had grown considerably, and by now Wink was acting as art director
for the big annual Lowlands Festival and for fashion
shows for the clothing label Diesel. Time for a new
logo. Above all, Wink wanted their new house style
to be musical and funky, in a modern way. And so it is.

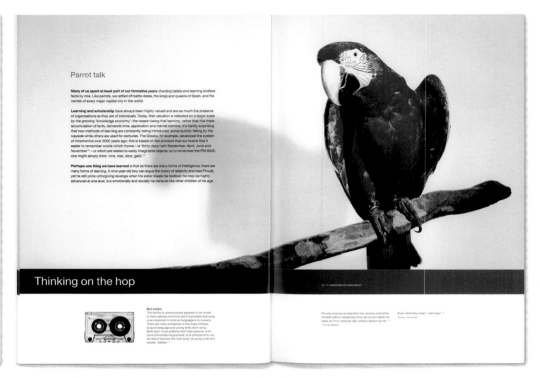

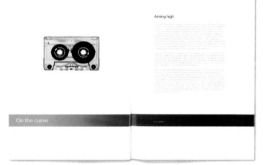

Thoughts and Everything Money Can Buy

The private investment bank Insinger de Beaufort serves a new financial elite – new money that often does not really feel at home in the established and conservative banking world. Han Bongers, director of communications at Insinger, accordingly felt that communications could be bolder than is customary in the traditional banking environment. In an advertising campaign by TWBA Campaign Company, for example, Insinger toyed with the standard image of the bored rich, such as a lady who goes to the psychiatrist with her Afghan hound – not to lie on the couch herself, but to have the dog analyzed. The punch line of the campaign was: 'You've got enough to think about'. Bongers had remembered Dietwee from their earlier BSO/Origin annual reports and asked them to take care of the Bank's annual report, line of brochures and website. He also asked Dietwee to enrich the slogan 'You've got enough to think about' with extra layers of meaning. A think tank was set up in collaboration with Aquarium Writers from London. For their first annual review, 'thinking', as the central denominator, was described from all sorts of perspectives; and in order to prevent the results from collapsing under the weight of pretension, the images play an associative, often slightly ironical game with the text. The typography is also intentionally reserved, in order to emphasize the understated tone. Although exceedingly modest, the annual review caused quite a stir in the banking world.

The website, in addition to offering corporate information and information about products and services, presents such amenities as an art gallery and a 'shop' which offers a selection of the priceless bizarre items that money (acquired through Insinger) can buy, such as a private two-seater submarine or extremely expensive Koi Fish.

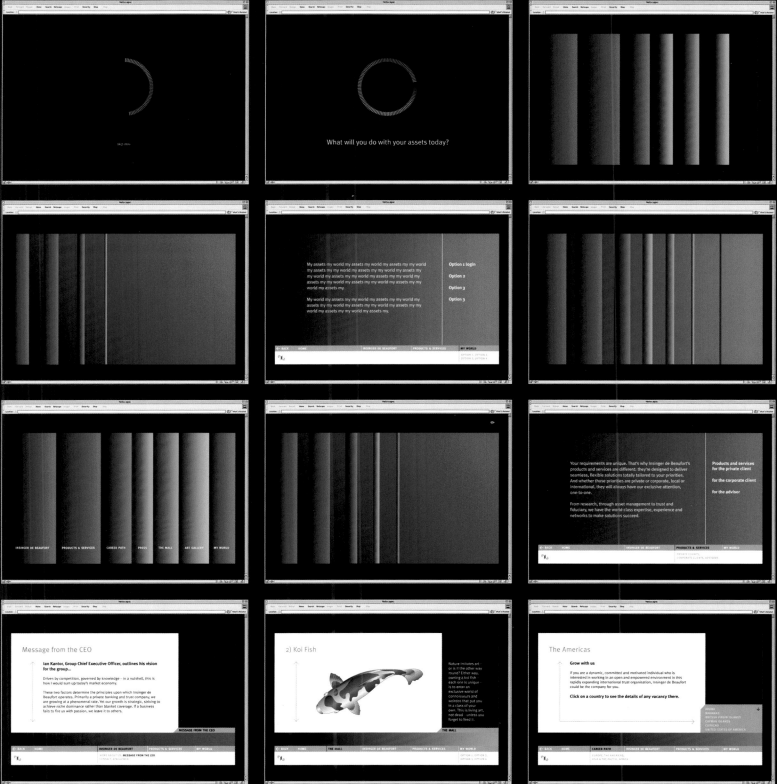

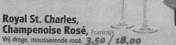

WIJNEN

HUISWIJNEN

Culemborg, Chenin Blanc, Zuid-Afrika, 2001/2002
100% Chenin Blanc, prettig droog en lekker fruitig. **2,50/14,50**

Culemborg, Cinsault, Zuid-Afrika, 2001
100% Cinsaultdruif, krachtige en volle smaak. Deze rode wijn.
past bij vele gerechten. **2,50/14,50**

Culemborg, Rosé, Zuid-Afrika, 2001
Net als de rode huiswijn gemaakt van de Cinsault. **2,50/14,50**

WITTE WIJNEN

Pinot Blanc, Dopff en Irion, Alsace, Frankrijk.
Zachte, soepele wijn van de Pinot-blancdruif.
Uitstekend bij vis, gevogelte en oosterse gerechten. **20,00**

Menetou Salon, Pierre Jacolin, Frankrijk, 2000
100% Sauvignon uit de Loire. Iets minder bekend dan
haar zusje Sancerre, maar zeker niet minder lekker!
De beste combinatie met geitenkaas. **25,00**

Viña MontGras Estate, Chili, 2001
100% Chardonnay, door overvloedige zon een diepe en
intense evan van tropisch fruit. Kan zeker ook met vlees. **18,00**

Tommasi "Viticoltori" Lugana, Italië, 2000/2001
100% Trebbiano di Lugana Veronese. Knisperend, vers,
harmonieus en plezierig. Heerlijk bij vis en pasta. **20,50**

Chablis 1er Cru, Simmonet Febvre, Frankrijk, 1999
Absolute top! Net als alle grote witte Bourgognes
100% Chardonnay. **34,00**

MOUSSERENDE WIJNEN

**Royal St. Charles,
Champenoise Rosé,** Frankrijk
Vrij droge, mousserende rosé. **3,50 / 18,00**

Veuve Amiot, Champenoise brut, Frankrijk
Droge mousserende wijn uit de Saumur. **27,50**

Pommery, Champagne brut, Frankrijk
Topchampagne uit Reims. **45,00**

RODE WIJNEN

Juliénas, Domaine D'Escuissin, Frankrijk, 1998/1999
Een van de mooiste cru's uit de Beaujolais.
100% Gamaydruif, veel fruit!
Ook gekoeld lekker bij wat lichtere gerechten. **25,00**

Saint-Emillion Grand Cru,
Château Montlabert, Frankrijk 1998/1999
Prachtige Grand Cru uit de Bordeaux. Veel Merlot en Cabernet-Franc.
Perfect bij rood vlees en wild. **35,00**

Rioja Tinto Crianza Cune, Spanje, 1999
Zes verschillende druivensoorten geven deze wijn
een mooie complexe smaak Krachtig! **21,50**

Sangiovese di Romagna Riserva,
Umberto Cesari, Italië, 1998
De 100% Sangiovesedruif en de rijping op Frans eikenhout
maken deze "warme" Italiaanse wijn tot een echte topper. **27,00**

Boschendal, Lanoy, Zuid-Afrika, 1999
Een blend van Merlot, Cabernet-Sauvignon en Shiraz.
Zeer fijne Zuid-Afrikaan, een allemansvriend! **27,50**

Speciaal aanbevolen

Koffie & Thee

Thee **1,50**
Koffie, Espresso **1,90**
Dubbele espresso **2,60**
Cappuccino,
Koffie verkeerd **2,20**
Irish, French of
Mexican coffee **5,40**

MARTINI

Aperitieven

Rode of Witte port,
Droge of Medium sherry,
Rode, Witte of
Droge Martini **2,40**
Campari **3,10**
Kir **3,60**
Kir Royal **4,60**

Zuivel

Melk, Karnemelk **1,60**
Chocomel **1,90**
Warme chocomel **2,20**
Warme chocomel
met slagroom **2,40**

Likeuren

Baileys, Amaretto, Cointreau,
Sambuca, Tia Maria,
Mandarine Napoléon **3,50**
Dom Bénédictine, Southern
Comfort, Drambuie,
Grand Marnier **3,80**

Frisdranken

Bitter lemon, Seven up, Sinas,
Soda, Sourcy blauw, Cola,
Cola light, Tonic, Ginger ale,
Cassis, Icetea, Appelsap,
Jus d'Orange, Fristi, druiven-
sap, tomatensap **1,90**
Verse jus d'Orange **2,30**
Solé mineraalwater
gassata/naturale (fles) **4,10**
Red Bull **4,00**

Digestieven

Louis Royer Cognac,
Calvados, Grappa **3,50**
Four Roses, Jack Daniels,
Armagnac **4,00**
Rémy Martin V.S.O.P. **4,60**
Courvoisier V.S. **4,10**

Tapbier

Amsterdammer **2,00**
Fluitje **1,90**
Seizoensbier,
Wieckse Witte,
Vos **2,50**

Whisky

Kilbeggan Irish Whiskey,
Burke & Barry's
Scotch whisky **3,40**
Four Roses, Jack Daniels,
Ballantines **4,00**
Glenfiddich **4,60**

Flesjes Bier

Amstel malt **2,30**
Gueuze, Kriek **2,50**
Duvel, Dubbel,
Triple, Sol **3,20**

Gedistilleerd

Oude of Jonge jenever,
Vieux, Berenburg, Jäger-
meister, Bessenjenever,
Apfelkorn **2,20**
Bacardi, Pernod, Gin,
Tequila, Vodka **3,40**
Bacardi Breezer (melon,
orange of lime) **4,50**

VERMAAK

Elke tweede zondag vanaf 16.00 uur

Tarde de Tango

Argentijnse tango, gelegenheid tot kijken,
luisteren en dansen in tangosfeer.
Org: Tangoschool El Gancho.
Tel: 030-2933608
De Grote Zaal. Entree gratis.

Elke eerste en derde zondag vanaf 17.00 uur

Salsamatinee

Dansen en dineren in salsasfeer.
Tapas in het Nachtrestaurant vanaf 16.00 uur.
Org: Union Latino-Americana. Tel: 030-2331154
De Grote Zaal. Entree met salsapas

Elke derde donderdag vanaf 20.00 uur

Café Latino

Open avond in het Café ter kennismaking
met Latijns-Amerika en de Spaanse taal.
Org: Union Latino-Americana. Tel: 030-2331154
Entree gratis.

Elke laatste donderdag van 20.30 - 21.30 uur

Politiek Café

Open discussies over actuele onderwerpen in het café.
Info: Harm Janssen.
Tel: 030-2620291
Entree gratis.

Elke woensdagavond vanaf 19.00 uur

Orakelcafé

Handlezingen en wijze voorspellingen in de Serre.
Org: Jacques Sontrop Tel: 030-2331778
Consult 10,00

Exposities

In de Kiosk en de vitrines door diverse kunstenaars.

Voor groepsreserveringen en informatie over verhuur kunt u
contact opnemen met het Polman's Huis, Tel: 030-2313368.

Salsa
Iedere maand in de Winkel van Sinkel!

Danslessen Salsa, Merengue, Son Montuno, Bachata
Cubaanse, Puertoricaanse of New Yorkse dansstijl.
Dansdemonstraties en eenmalige dansworkshops
Spaanse en Portugese taalcursus op diverse niveaus.

www.unionsalsa.nl e-mail st.union@wxs.nl
Tel. 030-2331154 - 06-53616666 na 13 uur

COLOFON

Dit is de lentemenukaart van de Winkel van Sinkel.
Geldig van april tot en met juni 2002.

Voor opmerkingen, reacties en reserveringen:
Tel: 030-2303030 Fax. 030-2303033
E-mail: info@dewinkelvansinkel.nl
Of schrijf: Oudegracht 158 3511 AZ Utrecht
www.dewinkelvansinkel.nl
www.nachtwinkel.nl

Openingstijden grand café-restaurant:
Maandag t/m zondag van 11.00 - 00.00 uur.
Clubavonden 00.30 - 05.00 uur.

Doordat wij met dagverse producten werken zijn onze
bereidingstijden wat langer en kan het voorkomen dat sommige
gerechten uitverkocht zijn. Hiervoor onze excuses.

Wij accepteren euro/master-card en pin.
U kunt ook pinnen bij de **ABN·AMRO** in dit pand.

Prijs- en kleurwijzigingen, alsmede drukfouten voorbehouden.
De afbeeldingen komen niet overeen met het daadwerkelijk
geserveerde menu.
Deze krant wordt gedrukt op 100% gerecycled papier.
Oplage: 50.000 ex.
Ontwerp: www.dietwee.nl

Winkel van Sinkel

Cultureel Culinair Warenhuis

OOK VOOR VEGETARIËRS!

LENTE 2002
(geldig van april t/m juni)

LUNCH

Meer dan een broodje

Kleffe witte broodjes zult u bij ons niet aantreffen! Wel serveren wij tussen 12.00 en 17.00 uur stevig belegde biologische boterhammen, klassieke salades, pasta's en warme gerechten. Natuurlijk ook voor zakenlunches en grote gezelschappen!

DINER

Van alle markten thuis

U kunt de gehele dag kiezen uit onze mondiale gerechten. Liefdevol bereid door onze chefkok en zijn keukenbrigade. Van Frans tot oosters, van voor- tot nagerecht. Vraag ook naar ons wekelijks wisselende 3-gangenmenu en de voordelige dagschotel.

DRANK

De hele dag lekker

Vanaf 11.00 uur bent u welkom in De Grote Zaal voor fris, koffie of thee (met de lekkerste appeltaart van Utrecht) en natuurlijk allerlei andere dranken. En als u echt iets te vieren heeft, kunt u Het Café afhuren voor een borrel tot 125 personen.

VERMAAK

Van tango tot house

Naast de zondagmatinees en de vaste clubnacht op zaterdag, gebeurt er natuurlijk nog veel meer in de Winkel van Sinkel. Hou dus naast de vaste activiteitenkalender (zie ook deze menukaart) onze site, de flyers, en de Uitloper in de gaten.

DE WINKEL VAN SINKEL: DE GROOTSTE, DE LEUKSTE, DE LEKKERSTE!

Gietijzeren vrouwen aan de Oudegracht

Anton Sinkel (1785) opende omstreeks 1820 zijn eerste zaak aan de Nieuwendijk in Amsterdam. Grote plannen had Sinkel ook met het oude St.Barbara- en St. Laurensgasthuis in Utrecht. Hij liet het hele complex slopen om vervolgens in 1837 te starten met de bouw van architect Pieter Adams' ontwerp. Het meest opvallend aan de Winkel van Sinkel, een neo-classicistisch 'winkelpaleis', zijn de vier grote vrouwenbeelden, gekleed in Griekse gewaden. Deze steunzuilen - kariatiden - werden per boot uit Engeland aangevoerd. De hijskraan bezweek onder het kolossale gewicht van een van de gietijzeren dames en viel met beeld en al in de Oudegracht. Het beeld overleefde het ongeval en de bouw werd voortgezet.

Deftig en gezellig

...verd de Utrechtse Winkel van Sinkel ...ter de manufacturenzaak bouwde ...et Neude een koetshuis in dezelfde stijl, ...kplaats en woning te dienen ...enburgstraat 19-21). Sinkel wilde dat ieder... ...a in zijn zaak thuis zou voelen en zorgde voor ...tige maar gezellige sfeer. Negen jaar heeft hij ...n florerende handel in Utrecht kunnen genieten. ...erleed in Amsterdam op 22 januari 1848. ...kel aan de Oudegracht werd door de erfgenamen ...het eind van de negentiende eeuw voortgezet..

...n unieke combinatie ...an cultuur en horeca

...8 verkochten de erfgenamen het winkel... ...n de bankiersfirma Vlaer en Kol, die in 1977 ...vergenomen door de Amrobank. Na de fusie ...e ABN werd het prachtige pand overbodig en ...d het een paar jaar leeg. In november 1995 ...de een nieuwe restauratie. Architectenbureau ...B kreeg opdracht het pand in de oude allure ...herstellen. Samen met architect Koos de Haan ...aakten zij het bankgebouw bruikbaar voor een ...eke combinatie van cultuur en horeca. Drie inter... ...tionale festivals vormen het culturele hart van de ...uidige Winkel van Sinkel: het Holland Festival Oude ...uziek, het Nederlands Filmfestival en Springdance. ...aast de regelmatig terugkerende culturele activitei... ...en biedt de Winkel van Sinkel kunstenaars gelegen... ...eid tot exposeren in een de ruimtes naast de ...rote Zaal. De exposities in de vitrines in de Grote ...aal worden verzorgd door Ron Ton Ton. Het koets... ...uis aan het Neude wordt momenteel verbouwd tot ...n Ticket- en Informatieshop.

Een begrip in Nederland

...0 augustus 1996, tijdens de opening van het ...ele seizoen, werd de 'nieuwe' Winkel van Sinkel ...l geopend door de burgemeester van Utrecht, ...telten. Naast de culturele voorzieningen en ...dcafé-restaurant in De Grote Zaal, vind je in ...l van Sinkel Het Café, De Serre, diverse ...een binnenplaats en een informeel, intiem ...rant in een van de werfkelders. ...is de Winkel van Sinkel net als in de ...eeuw een begrip in Nederland geworden. ...aren viel er regelmatig in de landelijke ...ver de Winkel. Over de zeer uiteen... ...e activiteiten, maar ook bijvoorbeeld ...ersuniformen die veel te kort zou... ...ijnlijk had Anton Sinkel dat ook ...vel de Winkel van Sinkel vandaag ...at minder deftig is als hij het ...n veelzijdig is het er zeker wel.

LUNCH *(van 12.00 tot 18.00 uur)*

BOTERHAMMEN

Gebraden lamsbout met jam van tomaat en chilipeper **10,50**
Boerenkaas **8,50**
Kip-mintsalade **10,75**
Gerookte runderlende met pesto **14,50**

Mozzarella en tomaat **13,50**
Gerookte zalm met verse kruiden **12,50**
2 Kwekkeboomkroketten **11,50**
Filet americain met kappertjes en ui **9,50**
Roerei met bacon **11,50**
Roerei met gerookte zalm **11,50**

SALADES

Gerookte runderlende met rougetsla en een crostino met tapenade **18,50**
Salade van aardappel met rougetsla, zalm en yoghurtdressing **14,50**
Caesarsalade van Romeinse sla met anjovismayonaise en parmezaanse kaas **14,50**
Salade van spinazie met feta en olijven **15,50**

WARME GERECHTEN

Dim sum (6 stuks, ± 15 min.) **15,00**
Quiche met broccoli en tomaat **9,75**
Spinaziesoep met croutons **9,50**
Dagschotel (iedere dag anders) **21,50**
Laksa pittige noedelsoep met zalm, taugé, paksoi en kokoscrème **12,50**

PASTA geserveerd met salade

Penne met gebakken tonijn en olijven, met een jus van tomaat en citroen **18,50**

Penne met champignons, pomodori, rougetsla en rode basilicum **18,50**

Vegetarisch

Penne met kip en amandelen in kerriesaus **18,50**

EXTRA ASSORTIMENT

Halve kreeft lauwwarm geserveerd met tomaat, basilicummayonaise en rucolasla **29,50**

Vast laag in prijs

Sushi plankje met een assortiment verse sushi **27,50**

Vraag naar de dagschotel en het weekmenu!!

"Graag uw speciale aandacht voor ons drie-gangenmenu!"

Kwaliteit staat voorop
Natuurlijk worden al onze gerechten dagvers en à la minute bereid, en via het wekelijks wisselende drie-gangenmenu kan ik u iets bijzonders aanbieden voor een zeer redelijke prijs. Een echte aanrader!!

Jan van Oeveren,
Chefkok

D'R BIJ *(koffie, thee of borrel)*

GEBAK

Brownie **4,50**
Truffeltaart **5,75**

Bananenroomtaart **5,50**
De Appeltaart **5,75**

IJSCOUPES

Cappuccino-ijs roomijs met cappuccino, dunne room en cacao **12,50**
Tutti frutti met vanille-ijs **12,50**
Sorbet sorbet-ijs met vers fruit, siroop en sodawater **12,50**

BITTERGARNITUUR

Dim sum (6 stuks, ± 15 min.) **15,00**
Dadels gevuld met kaascreme **6,50**
Sambalnoten* **4,50**
Bitterballen **7,50**
Olijven en feta* **5,50**
Vlammetjes **8,50**

*ook na 22.00 uur te verkrijgen

DINER *(van 18.00 tot 22.00 uur)*

VOORGERECHTEN

Gebakken gamba's
op roerbakgroenten, afgeblust
met oestersaus **21,50**

Loempiaatjes van tonijn
op ijsbergsla en taugé **18,50**

Dim sum (6 stuks, ± 15 min.) **15,00**

Stoofpotje van mosselen
met koenjit, venkel, knoflook
en paddestoelen **14,50**

Carpaccio van ganzenborst
op wilde spinazie met mosterddressing **19,50**

SOEPEN

Laksa pittige noedelsoep met zalm, taugé,
paksoi en kokoscrème **12,50**

Linzensoep
van rode linzen en room **9,50**

SALADES

Gerookte runderlende
met rougetsla en een crostino met tapenade **18,50**

Salade van aardappel
met rougetsla, zalm en yoghurtdressing **14,50**

Caesarsalade van Romeinse sla met
anjovismayonaise en parmezaanse kaas **14,50**

Salade van spinazie
met feta en olijven **15,50**

PASTA *geserveerd met salade*

Penne met champignons,
pomodori, rougetsla en rode basilicum **18,50**

Penne met gebakken tonijn
en olijven, met een jus van
tomaat en citroen **18,50**

Penne met kip
en amandelen in kerriesaus **18,50**

EXTRA ASSORTIMENT

Halve kreeft lauwwarm geserveerd met
tomaat, basilicummayonaise en rucolasla **29,50**

Vast laag in prijs

Sushi plankje met
een assortiment verse
sushi **27,50**

HOOFDGERECHTEN

VISGERECHTEN

Roodbaarsfilet
in de oven gegaard met een kruidenkorstje
en witte-wijnsaus **32,50**

Gegrilde zwaardvis met roerbakgroenten,
een paprikacoulis en couscous **32,50**

In terriyaki gemarineerde zalmfilet
met Chinese broccoli, sobanoedels
en komkommerpickle **29,50**

DE LANGSTE SUPERVISOR

"De Winkel van Sinkel is de
leukste zaak met het lekkerste
eten in Utrecht. Ik kom hier
zelfs in mijn vrije tijd!" *(Taco Albertsma)*

VEGETARISCHE GERECHTEN

Citroengrasrisotto met venkel **25,50**

Tutti frutti met in philodeeg
verpakte geitenkaas **25,50**

Roerbakschotel van groenten,
oestersaus en gemarineerde tofu **25,50**

DAGSCHOTEL

21,50

WEEKMENU

(3 gangen) **49,50**

Los te verkrijgen:
Voorgerecht **14,50**
Hoofdgerecht **30,50**
Nagerecht **12,50**

VLEESGERECHTEN

**Op herfstgroenten gebraden
kippetje** met gebakken Chinese kool,
sojasaus en Vlaamse frieten **32,50**

Lamscarré met gele curry
en in tempura gefrituurde groente **34,50**

Runderlende
met gegrilde groente
en Vlaamse frieten **34,50**

KINDERMENU *voor 12 jaar en jonger*

Kwekkeboomkroket
met friet en appelmoes **12,50**

NAGERECHTEN

De Appeltaart met vanille-ijs **9,50**

Yoghurt-dragonparfait
met een kletskop **12,50**

Notentaartje met vijgencompote **12,50**

Kaasplankje
met diverse soorten Franse kaas **17,50**

Cheesecake
met gemarineerd rood fruit **14,50**

IJSCOUPES

Cappuccino-ijs
roomijs met cappuccino,
dunne room en cacao **12,50**

Tutti frutti
met vanille-ijs **12,50**

Sorbet sorbet-ijs met vers
fruit, siroop en sodawater **12,50**

GEBAK

Brownie **4,50**

Truffeltaart **5,75**

Bananenroomtaart **5,50**

De Appeltaart **5,75**

OM DE ENORME BELANGSTELLING TE SPREIDEN RADEN WIJ U AAN TIJDIG TE RESERVE

Imagineering identity

After five years, Tinker Imagineers, specialists in developing and conveying ideas, had carved out a clear niche in the market. By now the company was selling its imagination to commercial enterprises, the government, educational programs and non-profit organizations. However, their common business house style, although effective, did not reflect the wilful way of working that Tinker had developed throughout the years. A new house style would have to unite both elements: businesslike, in order to retain the confidence of large institutional clients, but also playful and inventive, in order to emphasize Tinker's creative approach. Both associations come together in the new logo. A sturdy Helvetica suggests reliability; and, by pushing the dot of the 'i' one position backwards, an unconventional word picture suddenly arises. It hovers above the 't' like a thought balloon. As the house style developed, that dot became an almost independent entity. It transformed into the head of a man, took on the appearance of a juggling ball, or represented an exchange of ideas between several people. Their whole story could be told with a dot. Period.

"...for us, themed design means bringing content to life. We create attractive stories about any conceivable subject. It is our mission to develop educational exhibits that are commercially viable..."

tinker imagineers
bringing content to life

tinker
imagineers

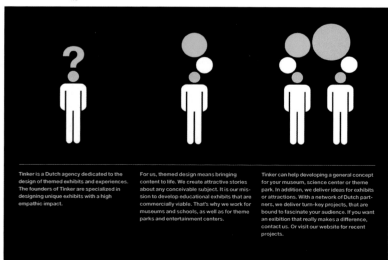

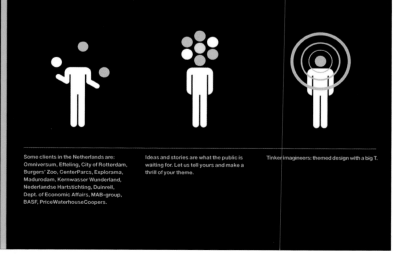

Tinker is a Dutch agency dedicated to the design of themed exhibits and experiences. The founders of Tinker are specialized in designing unique exhibits with a high empathic impact.

For us, themed design means bringing content to life. We create attractive stories about any conceivable subject. It is our mission to develop educational exhibits that are commercially viable. That's why we work for museums and schools, as well as for theme parks and entertainment centers.

Tinker can help developing a general concept for your museum, science center or theme park. In addition, we deliver ideas for exhibits or attractions. With a network of Dutch partners, we deliver turn-key projects, that are bound to fascinate your audience. If you want an exhibition that really makes a difference, contact us. Or visit our website for recent projects.

Some clients in the Netherlands are: Omniversum, Efteling, City of Rotterdam, Burgers' Zoo, CenterParcs, Explorama, Madurodam, Kernwasser Wunderland, Nederlandse Hartstichting, Duinrell, Dept. of Economic Affairs, MAB-group, BASF, PriceWaterhouseCoopers.

Ideas and stories are what the public is waiting for. Let us tell yours and make a thrill of your theme.

Tinker imagineers: themed design with a big T.

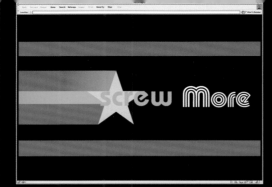
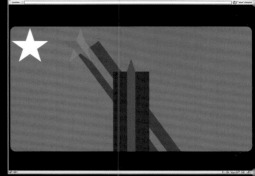

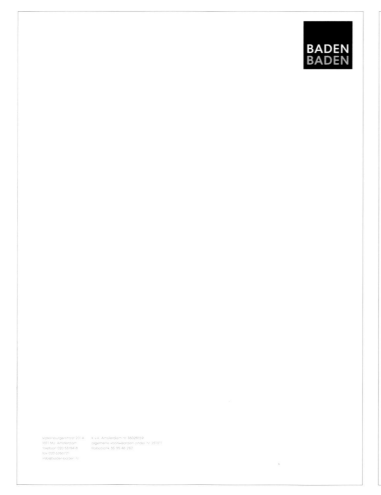

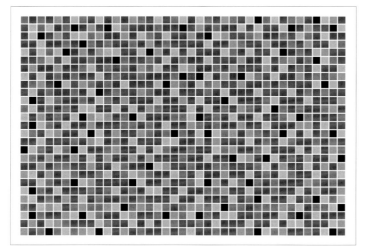

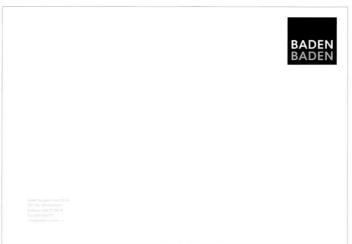

Minimalism

'Baden Baden' (which refers to baths, bathing, and a health spa resort in Germany) sells bathroom articles in the highest echelon of the market. Behind the concept of the store is highly experienced interior designer Piet Boon, whose window displays for Baden Baden equally call attention to his strict, minimalist approach to the interior. The house style also had to transmit that quality. The smallest bathroom element was eventually chosen as the basis of the design: the wall tile.

69 As An Impossible Figure

A visual representation of the number 69 was totally out of the question, and yet that number is recognizable in the final design. The initiators of Alpha 69, producers of music programs and events, especially desired a rythmical logo, that at the same time did justice to their attempts to convert the music festival format into television. The result is an image that refers as much to the impossible figures of M.C. Esscher as to the input signal of an amplifier and the winding of an audio tape.

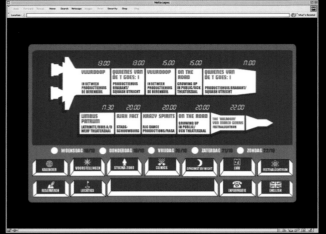

Sixties Sci-fi

Communications surrounding the youth festival
De Opkomst in 2000 associated the meaning of the
word 'opkomst' (used in previous festival editions in
the sense of 'up and coming') with the concept of

'launching'. The change of style in the printed material
and the website was chiefly determined by a new
and different aesthetic: space age, but then from the
more theatrical sixties point of view, varying from films

like James Bond to Barbarella. The website, completely made in HTML, adopted this visual language
by means of a 'chunky keyboard' in a navigational
structure that once again determined the design.

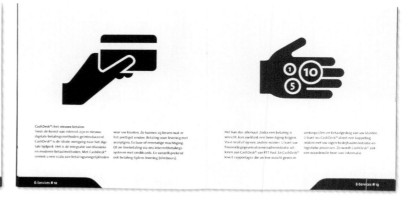

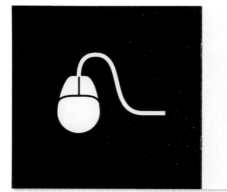

Business to Business

PTT Post (the Dutch national postal service) is primarily perceived as serving the consumer market by delivering letters and packages to homes. The re-styling of PTT Post's identity (by Studio Dumbar) initially underscored that image by introducing playful graphical elements based on parts of envelopes, which were to be used as illustrative bits and pieces in all means of communication. In reality, however, 80% of PTT Post's activities are in the business world. The new house style was less effective in that market – the reason why ad agency FHV/BBDO's creative director David Snellenberg and design strategy director Dingeman Kuilman asked Dietwee to investigate how a simplification of PTT Post's house style might enhance communication possibilities with the business world.

Dietwee advised that white become the most important 'colour' for PTT Post's business communications, and limited the red and blue to a supportive role in the play of typography and illustrations. Dietwee also advised that another style of photography with more clarity be used in brochures and PTT communications, and suggested a pictogram style which FHV/BBDO could use for the advertisements and billboards. The service offered by PTT Post in the business sector is fairly versatile and complex: statistical and communicative support, direct-mail services, printing-on-demand. All of these involve providing the most effective connection between sender and receiver, from A to B. The final design translated that into its simplest form. However familiar the use of pictograms may be in certain sectors of the design world, in the postal handling market it proved an effective innovation. Dietwee designed brochures, billboards, advertisements and the internet business portal 'www.wijzorgenervoor.nl'. Ultimately, of course, Studio Dumbar adopted the changes and resumed the development of PTT's business house style.

Ik blijf gezond

Verslag en visie 1999 / 2000

ONVZ

Gezondheid is je kostbaarste bezit. Dat is niet alleen het motto van ONVZ: de meeste mensen zijn zich hiervan bewust. En zoveel mensen als er zijn, zoveel ideeën zijn er over hoe je het beste gezond kunt blijven.

In Verslag en visie 1999/2000 laten we een greep uit deze uiteenlopende ideeën zien. Wat doet u om uw kostbaarste bezit gezond te houden?

Wetenschappers hebben ontdekt dat muizen in tredmolens niet alleen hun spieren, maar ook bepaalde hersencellen beter ontwikkelen. Dat kan betekenen dat sporters slimmer worden, vergeleken met luiaards.

Toelichting

Heel veel mensen drinken hun urine of smeren zich ermee in.
Er schijnt een heilzame kracht vanuit te gaan die allerlei ziekten kan voorkomen of genezen.

Ik blijf gezond want ik drink urine

Onze urine bevat belangrijke stoffen als minerale zouten, hormonen, zuren, vitaminen en enzymen. Urine zou volgens voorstanders kankervorming kunnen remmen en de weerstand doen toenemen.

Ontwikkelingen
in de zorgbranche

Een omgeving
zonder natuurlijke
elementen
veroorzaakt stress.
Door in de natuur
te verblijven,
wordt ons welzijn
op een positieve
manier beinvloed.

ONVZ in 1999

Slaapexperts bepleiten de revival van
het hazenslaapje. Dit half uurtje plat
moet bij voorkeur na de lunch.
Kantoormedewerkers gaan na het
middagdutje weer vol energie aan
de slag. Maar dit dutje mag niet langer
dan een half uur duren, anders val je
in een diepe slaap waaruit het moeilijk
ontwaken is.

Balans per 31 december 1999

Veel mensen
mediteren
om geestelijke
en lichamelijke
stress te verlichten.
Het monotone
zingen van het
woord 'om'
is daarbij een
bewezen middel.

Marktontwikkelingen
en plannen ONVZ voor 2000

Een konijn op doktersrecept?
Uit onderzoek blijkt dat huisdieren
een goede invloed hebben op de
gezondheid van hun baasjes.

Ik blijf gezond want ik heb een huisdier

Floaters, Piss Drinkers and Other Healthy People

After three consecutive annual reviews in the same format, health insurer ONVZ wanted a change of style. No more hard covers; and a horizontal format, preferably, in order to further surprise those who received the reports. The designers were reluctant to do so, because they believed that the element of surprise should be the concept and its content, and they preferred to keep the series intact. However, after some discussion they resigned themselves to ONVZ's decision to break off the series. They then presented ONVZ with a concept which for a health insurer was quite controversial. 'Ik blijf gezond' ('I Keep Myself Healthy') presents the alternative lifestyles people follow in order to maintain their health. Laughing, meditating, keeping pets, floating or even drinking urine.

Again ONVZ showed their remarkable ambition to stand out amongst other health insurance companies, not only in means of quality but in mentality as well. Dietwee asked photographer Vivianne Sassen to interpret these highly individual therapies in her own associative and poetic manner. In the annual report her images, accompanied by short explanatory texts and interesting facts related to health, are completely interwoven with the financial report, which was designed for the first time by Dietwee's designer Anke van Haarlem.
It was the fourth time that an annual review by Dietwee was included in the yearly Dutch '50 Best Books Awards', which was remarkable as these awards are rarely awarded to annual reviews.

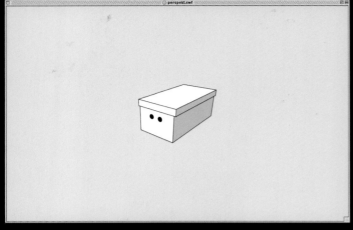

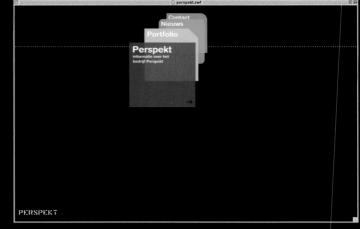

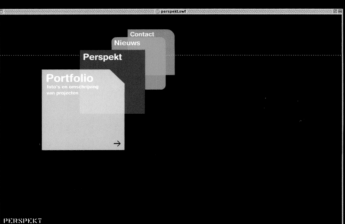

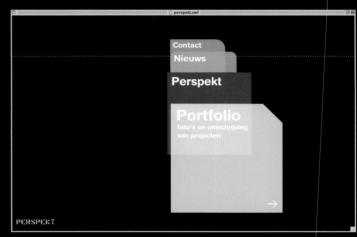

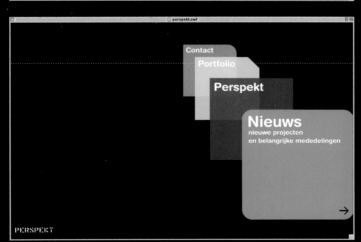

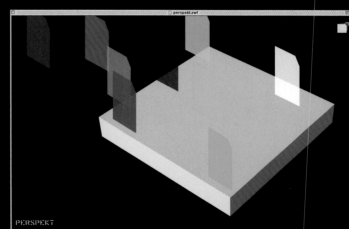

Three Dimensional Experience

Perspekt Studios can not easily be categorized. They originally came from a theatrical background of technical and experimental stage designers, but during the last twenty years they have become a company which designs sets for television, theatre and films, and also develops concepts, design and interiors for exhibitions, museums, expo's and conferences. Not only are they responsible for the concept and design, but also for the actual construction of the project, both in their own studios and on location. Perspekt Studio's came to Dietwee because they wanted a special website that would use the possibilities of the Internet in the same unusual and surprising manner as Perspekt strives for in their own three dimensional designs. Although the function of the site was to provide news and information about the company and to show a selection of their work, Perspekt wanted a visit to the site to be an experience in its

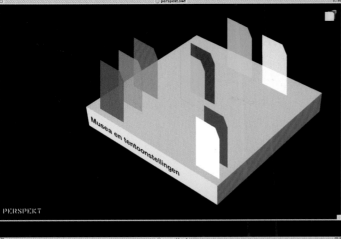

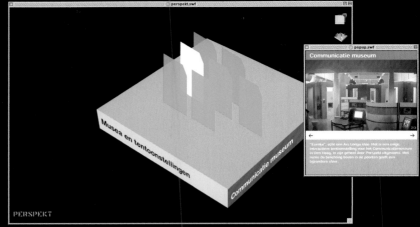

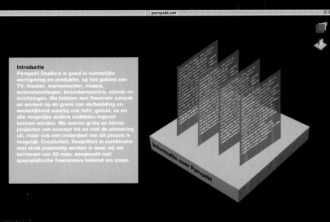

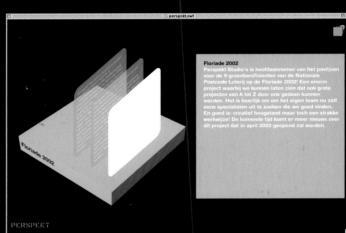

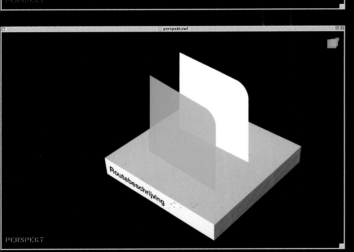

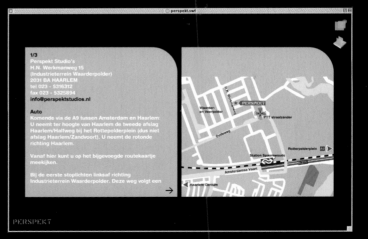

own right as well, so that implicitly the character and quality of their company would be expressed.

By looking through a peephole in a shoebox, Dietwee leads the visitor to a virtual black space where one finds sliding panels which move left and right and backwards and forwards upon movement of the mouse.

After having chosen where to go to, a three-dimensional theatre stage appears, with content suggested by sliding panels, representing information that can be reached by a mouse-click, after which a pop-up screen appears. By using their own two-dimensional graphic means, Dietwee has thus managed to make

a visit to Perspekt.nl a three-dimensional web experience with surprising simplicity.

Although the site is built entirely in Flash, access is quick, and a tool was provided for Perspekt so that they can keep the information up to date themselves without having to know how to use Flash.

ma	di	wo	do	vr	za	zo
01	**02**	**03**	**04**	**05**	**06**	**07**
C24 M41 Y45 K0	C4 M57 Y78 K1	C15 M56 Y73 K6	C2 M53 Y67 K0	C18 M68 Y80 K6	C14 M74 Y78 K1	C32 M46 Y55 K1
08	**09**	**10**	**11**	**12**	**13**	**14**
C29 M32 Y36 K0	C4 M67 Y76 K0	C12 M49 Y61 K6	C9 M45 Y58 K4	C13 M52 Y58 K4	C2 M72 Y47 K0	C15 M77 Y84 K1
15	**16**	**17**	**18**	**19**	**20**	**21**
C29 M31 Y33 K0	C2 M89 Y95 K0	C12 M46 Y54 K7	C24 M52 Y64 K9	C7 M46 Y58 K1	C2 M72 Y76 K0	C12 M73 Y80 K0
22	**23**	**24**	**25**	**26**	**27**	**28**
C41 M10 Y13 K0	C15 M61 Y64 K0	C15 M35 Y38 K0	C35 M66 Y75 K9	C3 M59 Y77 K0	C1 M83 Y87 K0	C4 M84 Y89 K0
29	**30**	**31**				
C44 M5 Y7 K0	C44 M5 Y7 K0	C29 M29 Y31 K0				

Ode to the Record Cover Girl

TDS Printers, a Schiedam-based printing establishment, sends a small desk calendar to their business relations every year. With each edition, they ask a different agency to make the design. 'The 365 Colours of 2001' was a hymn of praise to the record-cover sweetheart. With a slow wink at the soft porn of the Pirelli calendars so popular in printing offices, Dietwee searched for and found the 13 girls on the covers of the Dutch 'Alle 13 goed!' LP records ('All 13 are Great!') from the '70s. Their erogenous zones are carefully concealed beneath little coloured 'censorship' blocks on which the days of the month are printed. The colours are stated in CMYK values, so that, like with a CMYK samples fan, a person receiving the calendar can place a colour order by telling the printer the corresponding day and month.

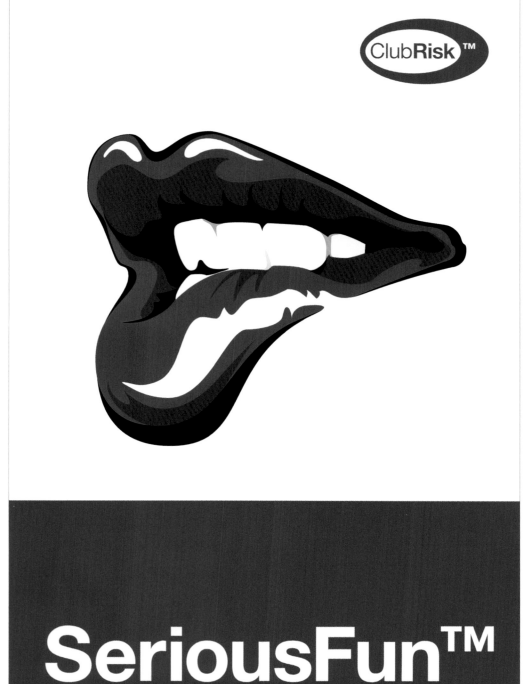

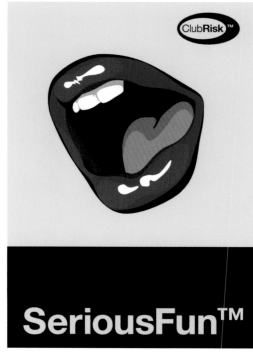

TM

What do you do when, after having opted to take a thematic approach in your publicity, you soon realize that this is not enhancing your brand name? You go back to the designers with whom you worked during the first successful period and ask them to restore brand name recognition. That's what Club Risk did. And Dietwee turned to methods that they had been using with increasing adeptness in corporate assignments: methodically building up a brand. Thus the language and ideas which they had developed in the corporate world penetrated into Dietwee's work for the nightlife scene, just as earlier it had been the other way around. With light irony, the slogans on the new Club Risk flyers and posters were presented as a registered trademark. The simplicity of the concept was a comment upon the gaudy circus of flyer designs, but it was also rooted in practicality. With an eye to the limited budgets and tightest deadlines possible for programming the nights, the design had to be simple and quick to produce at the very last minute.

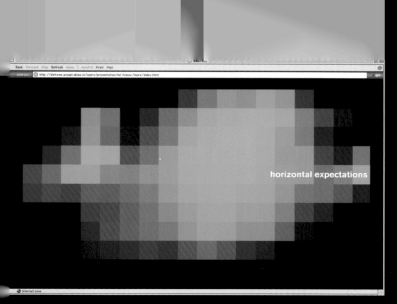

Façade

Sometimes a few months is enough time to strip down a multi-storied office building to its concrete skeleton and give it a different façade to make it contemporary. That is exactly what happened, in fact, with the re-launching of the Club More… website. The nightclub's new creative director felt that the original site was too funky for the extremely varied program at this Amsterdam night spot, which varies from Techno and Soulful House to Speed Garage, Two Step and heavy Jungle. Dietwee's web designer Lütsen Stellingwerf decided that there was nothing much wrong, however with the site's engine and fundamental structure which he had conceived for the previous version. Its system of page design left room for changing basic forms, which meant that the cosmetic layer could be totally

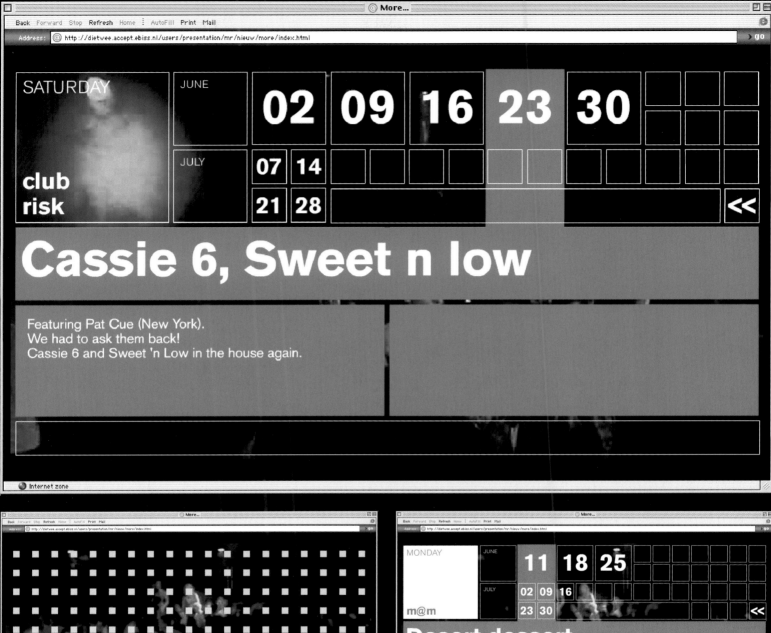

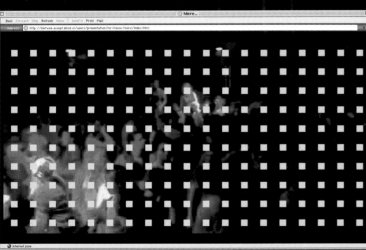

changed with relatively few interventions, and a great deal of the previous work could be saved. The biggest change, in fact, was that the round forms became

various nights on the program to express their own identity. With the site's changing background photos and music clips from specific nights, visitors now get

ontwerp: jorgen (www.dietwee.nl)

**BIKEMESSENGERS.NL
EUROPEES
KAMPIOENSCHAP
FIETSKOERIEREN
2•3•4 JUNI 2001
SCHIEHAVEN•ROTTERDAM
WWW.BIKEMESSENGERS.NL**

Grunge on Wheels

In the spring of 2001, bicycle couriers from all over Europe came to Rotterdam's
Schiehaven harbour to compete (in the pouring rain, unfortunately) for their
European Championship. The event – organized by an ex-courier under the aus-
pices of Rotterdam Cultural Capital – would be announced through a poster and
a website. The style was entirely determined by the completely idiosyncratic culture
of the bicycle-courier world: a freebooter's environment best compared in musical
terms with Grunge. Raw and selfish, but also full of specific humour and professional pride. Every text on the website folds out of an envelope accompanied by
the ringing sound of a bicycle bell. Jorgen Koolwijk, the Dietwee designer responsible for the design of the festival, had at one time been a courier himself.

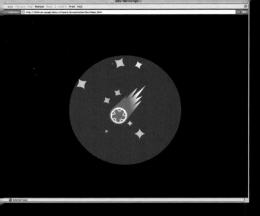
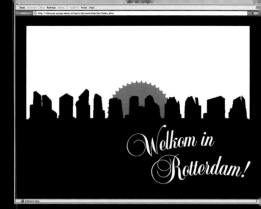

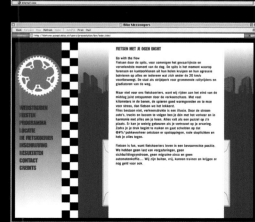

FIETSEN MET JE OGEN DICHT

Go with the flow
Fietsen door de spits, voor sommigen het gevaarlijkste en
vervelendste moment van de dag. De spits is het moment waarop
forensen en kantoorklanten uit hun holen krijgen en hun agressie
botvieren op alles en iedereen wat zich onder de 20 km/u
voortbeweegt. De stad als strijdperk van prommende rallyrijders en
gladiatoren van de weg.

Maar niet voor ons fietskoeriers, want wij rijden aan het eind van de
middag juist ontspannen door de verkeerschaos. Met veel
kilometers in de benen, de spieren goed warmgereden en te moe
voor stress, dan fietsen we het lekkerst.
Files bestaan niet, verkeersdrukte is een illusie. Door de stroom
auto's, trucks en bussen te volgen ben je één met het verkeer en in
harmonie met alles om je heen. Alles valt als een puzzel op z'n
plaats. Er kan je weinig gebeuren als je vertrouwt op je ervaring.
Zodra je je druk begint te maken en gaat schelden op dat
@#%*pokkeverkeer ontstaan er opstoppingen, rode stoplichten en
heb je alles tegen.

Fietsen is fun, want fietskoeriers leven in een bevoorrechte positie.
We hebben geen last van vergaderingen, geen
sickbuildingsyndroom, geen migraine-circo en geen
automatenkoffie…. Wij zijn buiten, vrij, kunnen trainen en krijgen er
nog geld voor ook.

NORTHSEA JAZZFESTIVAL 2001

13, 14 AND 15 JULY 2001
NETHERLANDS CONGRESS CENTRE
THE HAGUE, THE NETHERLANDS

Octopeller

For almost 30 years, the Hague embraces the jazz elite of the world during the summer. The North Sea Jazz Festival has become a household word for musicians and jazz lovers. With a special poster, organizer Mojo especially wants to cater to the festival's visitors, who can take it home as a souvenir. Dietwee submitted two proposals: a version with an octopus and another with a ship's propeller. Maritime associations both, but Mojo much preferred the propeller, because it best represented the styling ambitions of the festival organizer. The orange colour of the propeller lends a Dutch flavour to the poster; the typography refers to the lettering on shipping containers. The sparseness of the image reflects that of early Blue Note albums.

Chinese Take-Away

Stijn Ghijsen photographed the clientele of a Chinese take-away. During the Naarden Photography Festival he displayed the photos in a Chinese take-away restaurant, and for the occasion Dietwee made a simple foldout booklet as documentation of the project.

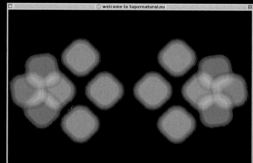

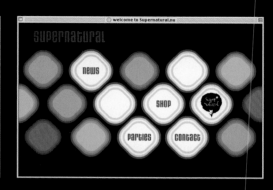

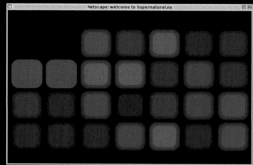

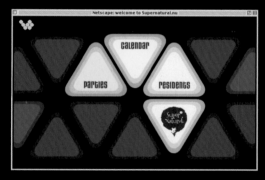

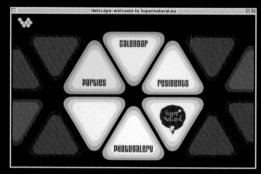

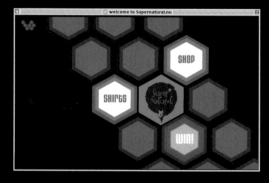

Disco Floor Navigation

At various locations in the Netherlands, Supernatural presents parties with a crossover from the earliest funk to music of the moment, but always based on a particular theme. The original designer for Supernatural, Taco Zuidema, came to Dietwee with its initiator, Michel Matthijssen, a.k.a. DJ Brownie, asking if they would be willing to build a website based on the present design for Supernatural's travelling concert

nights. Here again the Nachtwinkel site was the reason why they had come to Dietwee, and perhaps it was just because of that fact, that after some initial conceptual struggles Dietwee's web designer Michiel de Vreede was finally granted the freedom he needed to come up with something special. The Supernatural site is in fact quite modest in size, but navigation takes place on a disco floor that lights up.

Night Flight to the Tropics

The title of this little event in the Winkel van Sinkel must be taken with a grain of salt, of course. It is not the Mediterranean that this club whisks you away to, but the music of tropical beaches: bossa nova and Latin jazz with a contemporary beat. Flyers and e-flyers kept Club Met's visitors posted on its Friday night travel offers, always including a cocktail on the house.

Hierarchy

For more than three years now, Dietwee has maintained the site of telecom provider Ben on a daily basis. New material is constantly being developed and the design regularly undergoes subtle re-styling. In 2000, Ben's website was nominated by the ADCN for navigational design. Competition, continuing corporate growth and an increased number of departments mean that at Ben it more and more often happens that different specials or ad campaigns have to be publicized simultaneously, all of them requiring space on the home page. To solve the imminent problem of hierarchy, a new home page that functions as a portal to different sites was developed. Roll your mouse over a particular section, and that icon inflates, while others shrink, thus solving the problem of flexibility within the grid structure of the site. One click and the visitor can surf to very different areas such as Ben Business (above), Ben Olympic or to Ben Fun (next page).

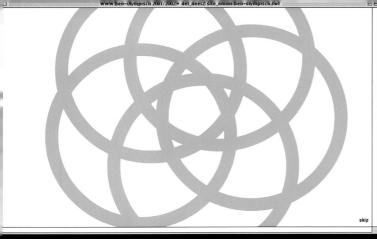

skip

Ben® olympisch

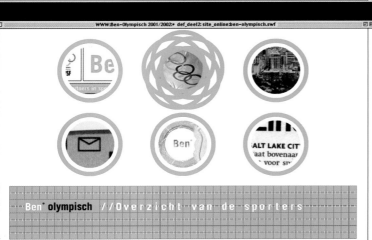

Ben® olympisch //Overzicht van de sporters

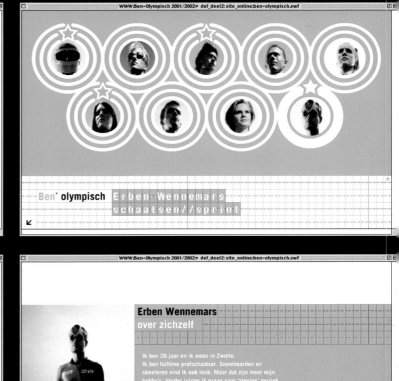

Ben® olympisch Erben Wennemars
schaatsen//sprint

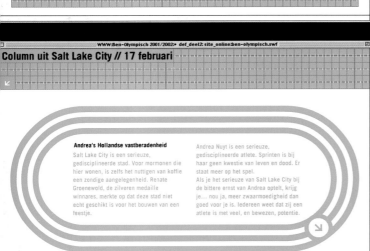

Column uit Salt Lake City // 17 februari

Andrea's Hollandse vastberadenheid

Salt Lake City is een serieuze, gedisciplineerde stad. Voor mormonen die hier wonen, is zelfs het nuttigen van koffie een zondige aangelegenheid. Renate Groenewold, de zilveren medaille winnares, merkte op dat deze stad niet echt geschikt is voor het bouwen van een feestje.

Andrea Nuyt is een serieuze, gedisciplineerde atlete. Sprinten is bij haar geen kwestie van leven en dood. Er staat meer op het spel. Als je het serieuze van Salt Lake City bij de bittere ernst van Andrea optelt, krijg je... nou ja, meer zwaarmoedigheid dan goed voor je is. Iedereen weet dat zij een atlete is met veel, en bewezen, potentie.

Erben Wennemars
over zichzelf

Ik ben 26 jaar en ik woon in Zwolle.
Ik ben fulltime profschaatser. Snowboarden en skeeleren vind ik ook leuk. Maar dat zijn meer mijn hobby's. Verder luister ik graag naar 'stevige' muziek. Van Pearl Jam via The Counting Crows tot De Dijk. Omdat ik het grootste deel van het jaar in het buitenland zit, is Nederland mijn favoriete vakantieland.

Olympics

As sponsor of the Olympic Games, Ben is closely involved with that sports event. The site reported on the Games with a mixture of fun and serious information and introduced the athletes sponsored by Ben. They introduced themselves in an informal way and commented briefly on the sport they practised and their expectations for the Games. Through an on-line quiz, visitors could win tickets for Salt Lake City; and during the Games, Ben customers could use SMS to play Lucky Day or the Toto based on the Olympic results and win prizes. The Olympic results could also be sent immediately to your phone by SMS. The site reported on the athletes' performances on the same day of the events, and announced when they were up next. After the Olympics the athletes published their

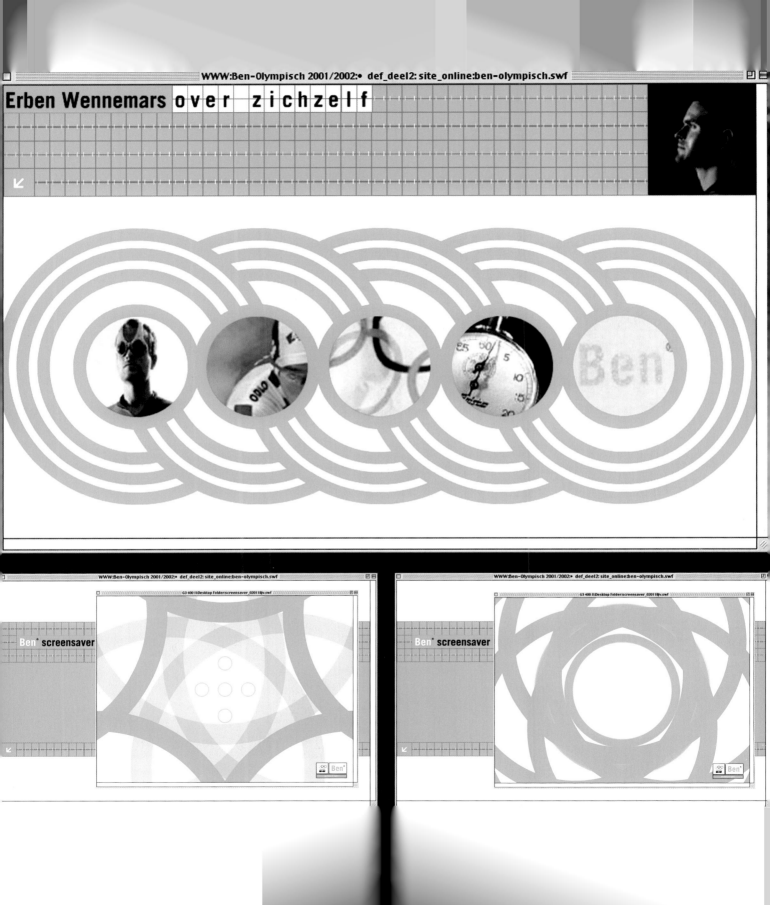

Erben Wennemars over zichzelf

Ben* screensaver

Ben* screensaver

Ben Fun

Theme sites such as Ben Olympic and Ben Fun add a bit of spice, both for visitors and for the designers, web editors and programmers who, after all, have maintained www.ben.nl day in and day out for some years now. Sub-sites based on either KesselsKramer's advertising campaigns or themes directed by Ben or by Dietwee provided them with the necessary design

variety and kept the site lively and up to expectations. Ben Pret (Ben Fun) is a place on Ben's website where Dietwee has developed a variety of e-cards, screen-savers and games which were often renewed, depending on themes such as Valentine's day, Mother's day, Easter, or, such as shown here, graduation, and which became extremely popular. There were also screen-

saver versions of these e-cards, which were built up from pen squiggles at real-time speed. With Ben, Dietwee proved that a brand can be both informative, effective and entertaining through creative use of the Internet. As mentioned before, from Ben's competitors only the very much larger KPN Telecom was visited more often on the internet.

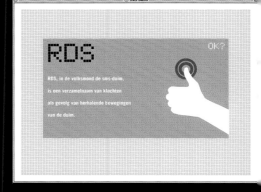
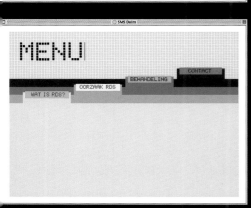
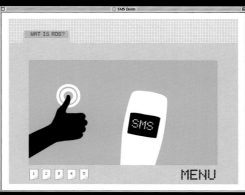
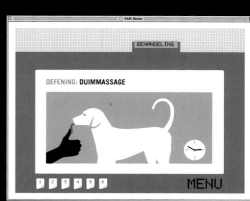

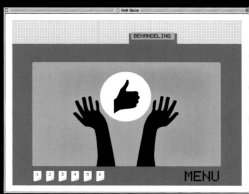

Rumour around a thumb

A good example of a sub-site based on the collaboration with Kesselskramer was www.sms-duim.nl, which translates as www.sms-thumb.nl). Johan Kramer made a 30 seconds film about the problems which arise from RTI as opposed to RSI. RTI stands for Repetitive Thumb Injury and is developed by too much use of mobile phones, and SMS in particular. RTI was offcourse invented by Kesselskramer but presented as a serious problem, by showing a girl with her thumb in bandages. More information could be found on the special website. The film was a commercial in disguise and meant as rumour around the brand. In the

film the voice-over (the trained listener could hear that it was the same as always used for Ben) did not actually mention anything about Ben. At the same time a big advertising campaign by Kesselskramers' Patrick van der Gronde and Pim van Nunen was launched. With a new Ben phone one could get two hunderd SMS-messages for free. The images in the campaign were of people with their thumb in bandages. Freecards were made showing people doing all sorts of strange things in order to treat and relax their thumb, such as giving it enough vitamine C by sticking your thumb in an orange. On the back the freecard referred to the

website; the only link in the entire campaign. On the site a lot of information, exercises and tips for RTI were found, some semi-serious, some very silly or funny. Deeper layers of information stated that the RTI problems arose because some telecom providers such as Ben had greatly reduced their SMS prices, making it thus very attractive to send SMS messages. That was the only link in the website which could be made to Ben. Apart from that it was unclear who the owner of the site was. The site was entirely conceived, written and designed by Dietwee's designer Jorgen Koolwijk and external copywriter Franklin Neuteboom.

What Creates Flow?

Unconventional, certainly in the established banking world. But that was exactly how private investment bank Insinger de Beaufort wanted its 2000 annual report to be. 'Rice is very difficult to understand' arose from a brainstorming session with people from Insinger and Aquarium Writers on the concept of 'flow': mastership generated with apparent ease. Many of Insinger's wealthy clients single-handedly created the fortune they entrust to the Bank, and perhaps they recognize, or would like to recognize, themselves in that profile.

In the annual report, Maarten Corbijn trains his camera on six masters of their crafts: a piano tuner, an interpreter, a flamenco dancer, an automobile designer, a diamond cutter, and a sushi chef (whose remarks inspired the title of the annual report). They tell about their motivations and their struggles for mastery which has

made them so outstanding. Insinger implicitly aligns itself with the inspiring values and qualities of their mastership.

The interviews were done by Aquarium writers. The design and typography is by Dietwee's Robin Uleman. The book is printed in four colours, but changing the fourth fluorescent colour for each quire created a much richer document.

Although the annual report received some internal criticism at the Bank (especially in the Channel Islands), 'Rice is very difficult to understand' was much appreciated by clients and won the Award for Annual Reports in the Netherlands and several communications awards in Germany and New York. Also, Insinger received a marketing award for the annual report from, of all places, Jersey and Guernsey. Mastership had also arrived in the Channel Islands.

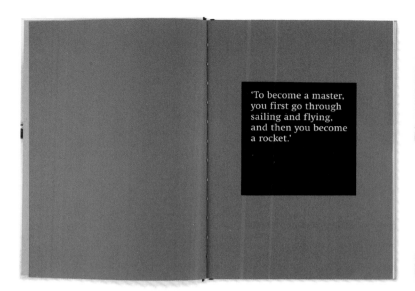

'To become a master,
you first go through
sailing and flying,
and then you become
a rocket.'

'Your first job, when confronted
with a new stone, is to be able
to assess its potential, to imagine
the biggest, the most beautiful
possible cut that can be extracted
from that particular diamond.'

Potential

The year 2000 illustrated the way in which our focus on people helps to create a productive framework. In the Far East, an initially modest presence in the region allowed us to develop an insight into the local opportunities. Accordingly, when presented with a widely dispersed target like Matheson, the offshore interests of the Jardine Matheson Group, we were well able to assess its potential. This depended on careful review, not just of the various organisations but of the potential and experience of key individuals. The picture was in many ways dominated by the interplay between 'old hands' and newer ones, as demonstrated by combining the resources of two new acquisitions, Jardine Matheson Trust

Company and Bramley and Co. Research and groundwork to achieve this complex and sensitive operation were laid in 2000, together with preparations to include Insinger de Beaufort's own Far Eastern presence. When all the elements are in place by early 2001, Insinger de Beaufort's trust business will have acquired local people in Hong Kong, Labuan (Malaysia), Mauritius, the British Virgin Islands and the Channel Islands – together with all the skills and experience it takes to make a comprehensive, integrated spread of jurisdictions ideally suited to the needs of today's globally attuned clients, not least in the burgeoning Asia Pacific region.

01_Passion

Our passion is for people. In a business that is all about service, they are key to success because service is ultimately about building a relationship – and then maintaining and nurturing it.

'When you choose fish, you can tell how healthy it is by looking at its eyes. If the eyes are clear and fresh, the fish is fresh; if they are cloudy and the scales are dry, the fish is not fresh. You also need to look at the body and the shape of the fish. If it is smooth and well proportioned – not lumpy or fatty – you know that this has been a healthy fish and that it will be perfect for cutting.'

'Flamenco has to be
in the heart. It's a
constant thing.
The more I feel, the
better I can dance.'

Individuals

In the year 2000, staff numbers grew from 602 to 920. At Insinger de Beaufort we don't just see that in numerical terms; through acquisitions or employment we were joined by 318 individuals, each with his or her unique background, skills and potential. It's a perspective on employees that we attribute to our insistence on delegating

HR matters to department heads, whom we expect to work closely with staff to ensure individual talents are given the chance to develop to maximum effect. An additional factor is the care with which we go about attracting, selecting and retaining staff.

'To become a master,
you first go through
sailing and flying,
and then you become
a rocket.'

'I had a quest to reach the top –
for ultimate knowledge and
ultimate learning. But, of course,
I realised that there is no top.
There is no end. The piano is
so complex, there is no end to
learning or training.'

'My training in Japan was so difficult that
it took me over a year to recover my health.
And even then, even after that training,
I knew that the tone I had found was still
not good enough.'

'The most important lesson I have learned is to be humble. To recognise that some people are better dancers than me, and that some are not. If I can keep my eyes open and see that others dance better, I can respect them.'

'Rice is very difficult to understand. It looks the same when it's dry, but once cooked the moisture needs to be exactly right – not too soft, not too hard. Once cooked and pressed, rice has a different texture. Weather affects the rice, so you need to watch the forecast. If it is hot, cooked rice gets hard and so it needs to be steamed for longer. If it is cold, it needs less water and steam. Also, rice picked at the beginning of the season is juicy and at the end it is dry. So the best rice is picked in the middle of the season. People think they can learn to cook rice in three years, but it takes at least five.'

'You need to keep an open mind. Whether something is good or bad, it doesn't matter. All that matters is that you learn and that you pass what you have learned on to other people.'

Group profit and loss account
for the year ended 31 December 2000

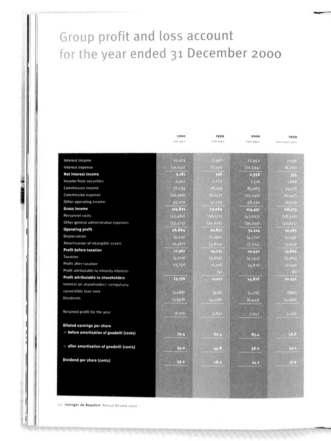

Group balance sheet
at 31 December 2000

Five year summary

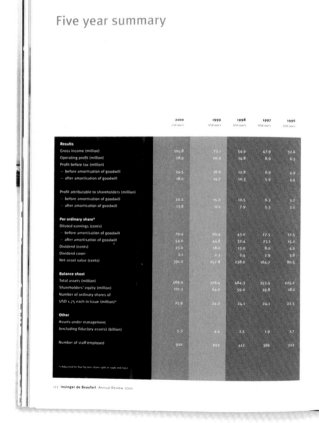

Gross income

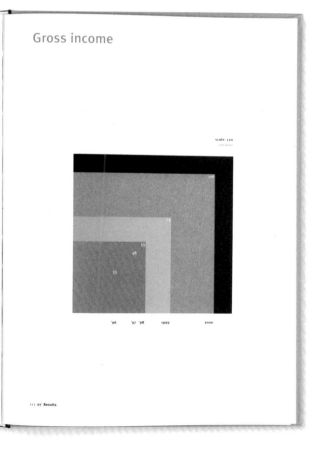

Tableau de la Troupe

'No friction, no spark' and 'No polish without a spit'. Dietwee greets their clients and the world under those mottos. Quite often the people from Dietwee reserve the right to come up with other ideas or to be a little tenacious. But how many of them are there, in fact? A Christmas card was the perfect way to introduce the whole studio. Under the ironic caption 'Dietwee can go climb a tree' – the silent groan of every client at least once, surely – portraits of all the employees were sent around. They can be pushed out of the card and hung in the Christmas tree like cardboard angels. A tree full of dedicated obstructionists.

Credits

A   Art direction
D   Design
P   Photography
I   Illustration
T   Text
C   Client
RF   Ron Faas
TF   Tirso Francés

9/11 The Verdict
Catalogue & poster: TF / Video wall: RF
Exhibition: Maura van Wermeskerken, RF, TF
supervised by teachers Ronald Timmermans
and Pieter Roozen of the HKU (Utrecht School
of the Arts) / P: Ligthart & van Aarsen
T: Hans-Onno van den Berg / C: BNO

12/13 Hardbop / BoomBoom
A: TF and Arne Koefoed (Wink) / D: RF, TF,
Harmen Liemburg, Michiel de Vreede
I+P: Various / T+C: Wink

14 Trunk-o-Funk
A+D: RF, TF / D: Richard van der Laken
T+C: Jungle Crew and Wink

15 Pretty Ugly Dance Company
A+D: RF, TF / P: Brothers Lumière
T+C: Pretty Ugly Dance Company

16/17 X Change
A+D: RF, TF / P: Patrice Molinard (cover)
T+C: Institut Français de la Mode

18/19 Stigters
A+D: RF, TF / D: Harmen Liemburg
P: Etienne Boyer / T+C: Stigters

20/21 Bridges
A+D: RF, TF / P: Various
T: Gerard Oostendorp, Theo van der Schaaf
C: BSO/Origin Nederland

22/23 Masterpiece
A+D: RF, TF / T: George Moormann (poetry)
P: stock / C: BSO/Origin

24/27 Dossier 94
Concept: RF, TF, Eckart Wintzen, Ron Meijer,
Birgitta Vos- Van Loon, Lisette Schuitemaker,
Meindert Slagter / A+D: RF, TF
P: People of BSO/Origin, Henk Tukker
T: Lisette Schuitemaker, Rik Smits
C: BSO/Origin

28/29 Cross Roads
A+D: RF, TF / D: Annelies Dollekamp
T+C: Institut Français de la Mode

30/31 Decisiveness
A+D: RF, TF / D: Richard van der Laken
P: Joost Meyer, Sjaak Ramakers
T+C: BSO/Origin

32/33 Filmtheatre 't Hoogt
A+D: RF, TF / T: Flavieke de Coninck,
Henk Camping, Petra Orthel, Arnoud Rijken
C: Filmtheater 't Hoogt

34/35 The GMD, a Product of Its Time
A+D: RF, TF / D: Annelies Dollekamp
P: Various / T: Elles Bulder / C: GMD

36 New Year's Eve with De Rebellenclub
A+D: RF, TF / D: Joanita van Haandel
C: De Rebellenclub

37 BoomBoom
A+D: RF, TF / P: Dixie Knight
T+C: Wink, Club de Ville

38/39 Commitment
A+D: RF, TF / D: Katja Berest
P: Various / T: Marianne van Blijenburgh,
Rinse Ebbes, Louis Alting
C: BSO/Origin Nederland

40 Jazz Radio
A+D: RF, TF / D: Tanja Kumpermond
C: Jazz Radio

41 Ex'tent
A+D: RF, TF / D: Harmen Liemburg
C: Ex'tent

42/43 Quadrant
A+D: RF, TF / D: Annelies Dollekamp,
Dylan Fracareta / I: Annelies Dollekamp
T+C: Quadrant communicatie

44 Get Stuffed
A+D: TF / D: Dylan Fracareta / P: Various
T+C: Ready Maids, Wink

45 New Year's Eve Winkel van Sinkel
A+D: RF, TF / C: De Winkel van Sinkel

46/49 Facts & Figures
A+D: RF, TF, -SYB- / P: Frans Jansen
T: Dietwee, -SYB-, ONVZ
C: ONVZ Zorgverzekeraar

50/51 Get Mixed Up
A+D: RF, TF / T: Taking care of music
C: FHV/BBDO, Stichting Drum Rhythm

52/53 Drum Rhythm Night
A: RF, TF / D+I: Dylan Fracareta
C: Stichting Drum Rhythm

54/55 Club Risk
A: TF / D: Dylan Fracareta
C: Club Risk

56 Yellowstone
A: RF, TF / D: Robin Uleman / C: Yellowstone

57 The Saloon
A: RF, TF / D+I: Robin Uleman / T+C: Moira

58/59 The Night Shop
A+D: TF / D: Robin Uleman, Jos Kluwen, RF
P: Robin Uleman, Jos kluwen
C: De Winkel van Sinkel

60 Supersonic
A: RF, TF / D: Robin Uleman
C: Club Risk, De Winkel van Sinkel

61 Welcome to the Future
A: RF, TF / D: Robin Uleman
P: Janna Hünnekes, Ellen van 't Woud
and stock / C: Club Risk

62/63 De Opkomst
A: RF, TF / D: Harmen Liemburg,
Robin Uleman, Dollekamp en Van Kampen
P: ANP and Various
T+C: De Opkomst/LOKV
(Dutch institute for art education)

64 Progracid
A: TF / D: Robin Uleman / T+C: Mike E

65 Summer Postage Stamps
A+D: RF, TF / C: PTT Post

66/67 Moondive
A: RF, TF / D: Robin Uleman / T+C: VPRO

68/71 25 Years 't Hoogt
A: RF, TF / D: Robin Uleman
P: Various / T+C: Filmtheater 't Hoogt

72/73 ONVZ Health Insurance Company
A+D: RF, TF / D: Anke van Haarlem
C: ONVZ Zorgverzekeraar

74/77 Your Most Precious Possession
A+D: RF, TF, -SYB-
T+P: Dietwee, Bianca Pilet
T+C: ONVZ Zorgverzekeraar

78/81 Dutch Design 1998-1999
A+D: RF, TF and -SYB-
(CD-Rom i.c.w. Keez Duyves, Harmen
Liemburg) / C: BNO, BIS Publishers

82/83 KPN Social Annual Report 1998
A+D: RF, TF / D: Herman van Bostelen
P: The Dutch Photographers, Onno Kummer
I: Robin Ulleman, Herman van Bostelen
T: CO2 (Joop K. de Vries and Bart van
Ratingen), Ruud van der Ros / C: KPN

84/85 Drum Rhythm Night
A: TF / D+I: Martine Eelman, Thomas Taris
P: Various / T+C: Stichting Drum Rhythm,
Mojo Concerts

86/87 De Opkomst
A: RF, TF / D: Anke van Haarlem
C: De Opkomst / LOKV

88/89 Origami
A: RF / D+I: Anke van Haarlem with
Esther van Gameren and Suzanne Nuis
P: Various / T: Jon Hoofwijk, Lilian Klijnstra
C: Origin Nederland

90/93 Moviezone
A: RF, TF / D: Robin Uleman
P: Various / T: Remco van Puffelen
C: Stichting Moviezone

92 Moviezone.nl
A: RF, TF / D: Michiel de Vreede
P: Various / T: Remco van Puffelen,
Angela de Kuijper / C: Stichting Moviezone

94/97 How is it going…
A: RF, TF / D+I: -SYB-, Martijn Engelbregt
Questionnaires: Martijn Engelbregt (EGBG)
T: Bakker en Voskamp
C: ONVZ Zorgverzekeraar

98 Ben
A+D: RF, TF / C: Ben Nederland

99 Ben.nl
A: TF / D: Lútsen Stellingwerf
T: Het Souterrain (Franklin Neuteboom)
P: Various / T+C: Ben Nederland

100/102 Ben.nl
A: TF / D: Marco Deijman,
Lútsen Stellingwerf, Dirkjan Brummelman,
Michiel de Vreede, Dirkje Bakker
T: Het Souterrain (Franklin Neuteboom)
P: Various / T+C: Ben Nederland

103 Ben Dealer.nl
A: TF / D: Dirkjan Brummelman
P: Various / T+C: Ben Nederland

104/105 Upclub
A: TF / D: Robin Uleman
C: De Winkel van Sinkel

106/107 Night Shop
A: RF, TF / D: Robin Uleman
C: De Winkel van Sinkel

108/111 Night Shop
A: RF, TF / D: Dirkjan Brummelman,
Robin Uleman / C: De Winkel van Sinkel

112/113 Choosing
A: RF / D: Martine Eelman
P: Yvonne Witte / T: CO2 (Joop K. de Vries,
Bart van Ratingen) / C: KPN Telecom

114/115 KPN
A: RF / D: Ivo de Boer, Martine Eelman,
De Designpolitie (Richard van der Laken,
Pepijn Zurburg) / P: The Dutch
Photographers
T+C: KPN Telecom

116/118 Knowing Everything About
A: RF, TF / D: RF, Ivo de Boer
P: Isis Torensma, Wieteke de Lange,
Judith van IJken, Niels Stomps
T+C: Hogeschool van Utrecht

119 HvU.nl
A: TF / D: Dirkjan Brummelman
T+C: Hogeschool van Utrecht

120 Factor H
A: RF, TF / D: Martine Eelman / C: Factor H

121 Wink
A: RF, TF / D: Anke van Haarlem / C: Wink

122 Something to Think About
A: RF, TF / D: Robin Uleman / P: De Studio
T: Aquarium Writers (Louise Hide,
Roden Richardson) / C: Insinger de Beaufort

123 Insinger.com
A: RF, TF / D: Robin Uleman
T: Aquarium Writers (Louise Hide,
Roden Richardson) / C: Insinger de Beaufort

124/127 Winkel van Sinkel
A: RF, TF / D: Jos Kluwen
P: stock / T+C: De Winkel van Sinkel

128 Tinker Imagineers
A: RF, TF / D+I: Robin Uleman
T+C: Tinker Imagineers

129 Expectmore.nl
A: TF / D: Lútsen Stellingwerf
T+C: Club More...

130 Baden Baden
A: RF, TF / D: Robin Uleman
C: Baden Baden

131 Alpha 69
A: RF / D: Rogier Bisschop
C: Alpha 69 Productions

132/133 De Opkomst
A: RF, TF / D+I: Jorgen Koolwijk
T: Barbara Lindenbergh, Hanneleen
Stratemeier / T+C: Festivalbureau Storm
at LOKV (Dutch institute for art education)

134/135 PTT Post
A: RF, TF / D: Robin Uleman,
I: Rogier Bisschop, Robin Uleman
T: FHV/BBDO / C: PTT Post

136/137 I Stay Healthy
A+D: RF, TF / D: Anke van Haarlem
with Suzanne Nuis / P: Vivianne Sassen
T: Dietwee / C: ONVZ Zorgverzekeraar

138/139 perspekt.nl
A: TF / D: Dirk-Jan Brummelman

P+T+C: Perspekt Studio's

140/141 The 365 Colours of 2001
A: RF, TF / D+I: Marjolein Spronk,
Martine Eelman / P+T: Various
C: TDS drukwerken

142 Serious Fun
A: TF, Robin Uleman / D+I: Rogier Bisschop
T+C: Club Risk

143 More... Club Risk
A: TF / D: Robin Uleman, Rogier Bisschop
T+C: Club Risk

144-145 Expectmore.nl
A: TF / D: Lútsen Stellingwerf
P: Various / T+C: Club More...

146 The New City Council Program
A: RF / D: Thomas Taris
C: Filmtheater 't Hoogt

147 Films, Churches and Organs
A: RF / D+P: Jorgen Koolwijk
(still from 'La passion de Jeanne d'Arc'
from Carl Theodor Dreyer)
T+C: Filmtheater 't Hoogt

148/149 Bikemessengers
A: RF, TF / D+I: Jorgen Koolwijk
T: Kuno Bakker / C: Buro Fris

150 North Sea Jazz Festival 2001
A: RF, TF / D: Robin Uleman
P: Vetus Den Ouden
C: North Sea Jazz Festival/Mojo Concerts

151 Take Away
A: RF, TF / D: Marjolein Spronk
P+C: Stijn Ghijsen

152 Supernatural.nu
A: TF en Taco Zuidema / D: Michiel de Vreede
T: Joep Beving / C: Supernatural

153 Club Met
A: RF, TF / D+I: Jorgen Koolwijk
C: De Winkel van Sinkel

154 Ben Portal
A: TF / D: Lútsen Stellingwerf,
C: Ben Nederland

155 Ben Business
A: TF / D: Dirkjan Brummelman,
Sandra Gianonne
T: Het Souterrain (Franklin Neuteboom),
Ben Nederland / T+C: Ben Nederland

156/157 Ben Olympic
A: TF, Dirkjan Brummelman
D: Dirkjan Brummelman, Michiel de Vreede
T: Het Souterrain (Franklin Neuteboom)
C: Ben Nederland

158 Ben Passed!
A: TF / D: Dirkjan Brummelman
C: Ben Nederland

159 SMS-Thumb
A: TF / D: Jorgen Koolwijk
T: Het Souterrain (Franklin Neuteboom),
Ben Nederland / T+C: Ben Nederland

**160/163 Rice is Very Difficult to
Understand**
A: RF, TF / D: Robin Uleman
P: Maarten Corbijn / T: Aquarium Writers
(Louise Hide, Roden Richardson)
C: Insinger de Beaufort

164/165 Dietwee Can Go Climb a Tree
Concept: Robin Uleman / A: RF, TF
D+I: Jorgen Koolwijk / P: Bas Wilken

Thank you...

... clients

Antoine Achten / Tim Akers / Daniëlle Albek / Fred Allers / Walter Amerika / Antoinette Andriese / Anutosh / Kuno Bakker / Sander Bakker / Erik Bär / Luc van Beers / Kirsten Bekkering / Aaron Betsky / Marianne van Blijenburgh / Han Bongers / Marjolein Bronkhuizen / Aad Boon / Piet Boon / Ton Boon / Stan Boshouwers / Frank Bottema / Jan Bouts / Anneloes Bouw / Bart Bruinsma / Ingrid van Buren / Dimitri van der Burgt / Henk Camping / Jean-Pierre Claes / Dagan Cohen / Iris Coolen / Johan Coops / Marie Helene Cornips / Frankie D. / Melle Daamen / Niek-Jan van Damme / Jan-Willem Dekker / Jurgen Dhollander / Tom Dorresteijn / Myra Driessen / Daniëlle van Duin / Mark Düthler / Mike E / Ariane Collot d'Escury / Kees Eijrond / Roeland Geertzen / Wil Giezenaar / Arvid Gustafsson / Gregoor van Gemert / Femke van Gemert / Kees Groothuis / Siebe Grijpma / Aad Faas / Hariëtte Haasen / Kevin Halouska / Michael Halve / Rita van Hattum / Henny van der Heiden / Pieter van der Heide / Sylvia Heimans / Ted van Hintum / Theo van den Hoek / Nancy van Hofwegen / Micky Hoogendijk / Saskia van der Horst / Hub. Hubben / Rob Huisman / Ron Huizer / Vincent Huizing / Jacobien Hummelen / Renate Hunfeld / Patrick van de Hijden / Maaike Jansen / Emiel de Jong / Ian Kantor / Astrid Karbaai / Frank Kempeneers / Hetty Keiren / Teus Kerkhof / Timar de Keijzer / Marcel Klever / Lilian Klijnstra / Suzanne Knotnerus- Klein / Pieter Kramer / Willem Koch / Arne Koefoed / Lidewij de Koekkoek / Willem Koot / Simone de Koster / Maurice Krabbenborg / Ad Krechting / Dingeman Kuilman / Jan de Kuiper / Wim Kuus / Angela de Kuijper / Onno Kwint / Joyce Langezaal / Huib van der Linde / Barbara Lindenbergh / Kim van der Loo / Ada Lopez- Cardozo / Godfried van der Lugt / Laurens Lijding / Muriel Maas / Eymert van Manen / Dave Mangene / André Matthijsse / Michiel Matthijsen / Remy Meijers / Stanja van Mierlo / Lucas Mol / Rob Mooy / Netteke Mijnster / Madelon Mijnster / Daniël Nicolaï / Cor Noltée / Harm Noordhof / Inge Noordijk / Iduna Nottelman / Marcel Oden / Petra Orthel / Hans van Os / Linda Osnabrug / Filip Otten / Rogier Paans / Bas van der Paardt / LX Pacific / Titika Papaikonomou / Frank Peek / Cynthia Pelman / Frank Philips / Frank Posthumus / Didier Prince / Gertjan Pruim / Stephan Tellier / Suzanne Tide- Frater / Cornelie Tollens / Polly van Raam / Jan-Paul Reij / Patrick Reijnen / Mike Richters / Jeroen Roeleveld / Marianne Rübsaam / Käthe Ruyssenaars / Frans van Rijn / Ed van Rijswijk / Rob Saltzherr / Werner Schrijver / Lisette Schuitemaker / Yvette Schul / Meindert Slagter / Steven Slings / Richard Smit / David Snellenberg / Gerben Snijder / Marja Souër / Arjan Steevels / Ed Stibbe / Edward Stolze / Hans van Straten / Lies Straub / Bennie Vaasen / Gert van Veen / Sjoerd Vellenga / Pieter van Velzen / Henk Verhoog / Julius Vermeulen / Paul van de Vlist / Koen Vollaers / Roland van der Vorst / Gerrit Vos / Wouter Vos / Birgitta Vos- Van Loon / Jan Willem Vosmeer / Paul Vossen / Maarten van de Vijfeijken / Mark Wassenaar / Olivier Wegloop / Claudine Weinstein / Douwe Werkman / Kirsten van der Wiel / Jan Wigmans / Dini Wildschut / Marcel van Wing / Eckart Wintzen / Daniëlle Wolvenkamp / Heleen van der Wouden / Frank van Wijk

... collegues and friends

Sander Bakker / Haico Beukers / Addie de Boer / Hugo Bos / Ronald Bos / Herman van Bostelen / Abel Derks / Karin van Duijnhoven / Ruud van Empel / Martijn Engelbregt / Femke van Gemert / Nikki Gonnissen / Patrick van der Gronde / Bart de Groot / Dick de Groot / Wilbert de Haan / Robert-Jaap Jansen / René Jaspers / Matthijs de Jong / Peter Jonker / Erik Kessels / Jacques Koeweiden / Anne Koningsberger / Johan Kramer / Dingeman Kuilman / Sybren Kuiper / Richard van der Laken / Pieter Leendertse / Harmen Liemburg / Gerbrand van Melle / Ron Meijer / † Derek Mobbs / Richard Niessen / Pim van Nunen / Paul Postma / Sandra Rabenou / Hans Rietveld / Pieter Roozen / Gerard Schilder / Engin Selikbas / David Snellenberg / Ronald Timmermans / Arno Twigt / Maarten van de Vijfeiken / Jann de Waal / Maura van Wermeskerken / Thomas Widdershoven / Mariek Witlox / Arjen Woudenberg / Pepijn Zurburg

... photographers

Chris Bonis / Etienne Boyer / Koos Breukel / René ten Broeke / Lard Buurman / Maarten Corbijn / Stijn Ghijsen / Jolanda den Harder / Frans Jansen / Marie José Jongerius / Alex Koeleman / Onno Kummer / Wieteke de Lange / Rogier Maaskant / Christiaan van Mameren / Leendert Mulder / Bianca Pilet / Sjaak Ramakers / Vivianne Sassen / Maurice Scheltens / Friso Spoelstra / Niels Stomps / Andre Thijssen / Isis Torensma / Johan Visschedijk / Hans Willemsen / Henk Wildschut / Yvonne Witte / Judith van IJken / Ton Zonneveld

...writers

Jane Bemont / Hans Onno van den Berg / Louise Hide / Jon Hoofwijk / Oda de Jong / Lilian Kleinstra / George Moorman / Toon Lauwen / Franklin Neuteboom / Roden Richardson / Mari Shields / Gert Staal

... printers

Jos van Beek / Hans Delfos / Frans Eijkenbroek / Bert van Heusden / Rinus and Rini Heijt / Hans Janssen Maneschijn / Bas Olthof / Leon Quaden / Cor Rosbeek / Rick Stekelenburg / Fokko Tamminga / Piet Thomas / Leonard de Vos / Joost Widdershoven / Erik Wink

... people from ROTIPERIKO

Yvonne Bartels / Pauline Pels / Arco Schuurman / Koen Verhagen / Milan Vis

... people who gave us advice

Kees van Alphen / Nick van Buitenen / Bart Bruinsma / Vincent van den Eijnde / Mathieu van Grafhorst / Gert van der Houwen / Robin Hulsbergen / Olav van der Linden / Bert Murk / Joost Oorthuizen / Jeroen Oudendag / Job van der Pijl / Gijs Verloop / Peter Vogelenzang

... all teachers from the HKU

specially; † Piet Bakker / Henri Lucas / Pieter Roozen / Ronald Timmermans / Wim Wal / Mart. Warmerdam

... BIS Publishers

Rudolf van Wezel / Willemijn de Jonge / Rietje van Vreden

... people who worked with us

Nadia Adrian / Ivo de Boer / Herman van Bostelen / Keez Duyves / Martijn Engelbregt / Collette van Essen / Paul Faas / Esther van Gameren / Veronique van Kampen / Sander Kessels / Sybren Kuiper / Richard van der Laken / Suzanne Nuis / Barbara Peerdeman / Thomas Taris / Pepijn Zurburg

... those who have worked over the past 13 years at Dietwee

Kerrie van Aarssen / Liesbeth Batelaan / Katja Berest / Marielle Berkelmans / Peer Boon / Kim Bruinsma / Marco Deijman / Annelies Dollekamp / Martine Eelman / Ernie Enkelaar / Guido Eijrond / Dylan Fracareta / Nashima Gokani / Anke van Haarlem / Eva van Hilst / Joanita van Haandel / Judith Hofland / Erik Hoogendorp / Martine Houthuijs / Jos Kluwen / Bianca Knijn / Melvin Kruin / Tanja Kumpermond / Teresa Küpfer / Wijnand Langen / Elles Lauer / Harmen Liemburg / Frank Lucas / Anne Middelkamp / Esther de Munnik / Pauline de Raadt / Thijs Remie / Krista Rozema / Arco Schuurman / Barbara Slagman / Alex Slagter / Roel Uleners / Gijs Verloop / Sanne Vogel / Michiel de Vreede

... Dietwee today

Dirkje Bakker / Rogier Bisschop / Martin Bos / Joseefke Brabander / Dirk-Jan Brummelman / Matthea Bussemaker / Marieke van Ditshuizen / Sonja van Eyken / Ron Faas / Tirso Francés / Sandra Gianonne / Jorgen Koolwijk / Maikel van der Laken / Andrea de Leeuw / Joep Modderman / Ernest Petrus / Marjolein Spronk / Lútsen Stellingwerf / Sander Tóth / Robin Uleman / Jan Willem van Veelen / Arlette van Vliet / Tabitha Vogels / Wim Volle / Bas Wilken / Liesbeth van Woerkens / Leone Zielhuis

... and specially

Mirjam Nijdeken and Katia Lucas